Reflections of Nature

THE
ART & EMBROIDERY
OF
Jane Hall

For Neil

I'd walk a thousand, thousand miles with you,

and never tire of our journey.

Close steps, clasped hands,

even when we're weary.

We'll delight in gentle things,

embrace the strength of great things.

If we get lost along the way,

we'll find ourselves in each other.

Reflections of Nature

THE
ART & EMBROIDERY
OF
Jane Hall

First published in Great Britain 2007

Search Press Limited
Wellwood, North Farm Road,
Tunbridge Wells, Kent TN2 3DR

Text copyright © Jane Hall 2007

Photographs by Charlotte de la Bédoyère,
Search Press Studios
Photographs of the artist by Neil McLean
Natural history photographs by Jane E Hall

Photographs copyright © Search Press Ltd. 2007

Design copyright © Search Press Ltd. 2007

ISBN-10: 1-84448-038-0
ISBN-13: 978-1-84448-038-8

The Publishers and author can accept no responsibility
for any consequences arising from the information,
advice or instructions given in this publication.

Suppliers
If you have difficulty in obtaining any of the materials
and equipment mentioned in this book, please visit the
Search Press website for details of suppliers:
www.searchpress.com

Alternatively, you can visit the author's website:
www.clothofnature.com
for a current list of stockists, including firms who
operate a mail-order service.

Reproduction by Altaimage London
Printed in Malaysia by Times Offset (M) Sdn Bhd

ACKNOWLEDGEMENTS

First I would like to thank my parents for their love
and support; in their nurture my life as an artist
was founded.

I would also like to acknowledge the love and support
of my family and friends. Like the wild flowers which
inspire my work, they are all beautiful and special
to me. Particular thanks to Jenny and Robert for their
love and quiet patience.

A sincere thank you to the team at Search Press,
especially to Roz, Katie and Juan who have worked
closely with me in accomplishing this book, their
support and encouragement never failing.

Special thanks to Lotti, for her skill and patience
photographing my work, and to Neil for patiently
accompanying me with heavy photographic
paraphernalia, cross country, to picture me
'on location'.

Thanks to my father, Freddie Hall, and Rob
Bull for their skill and patience over the years in
accomplishing the framing and presentation of
my work.

Particular thanks are extended to the owners of
various works illustrated: Joan Benson, Jan and Patrick
Bourke, Susan Classen, James Escombe, Margaret
Escombe, Theony and Chris Lianas-Greenwood,
Gwen Russell and Judy Weston. Thanks also to Fiona
and Peter Bourke who gave their kind permission for
the studio location photography.

Thanks to Neil, and Fiona Bourke for their help in
typing up my text. I would also like to thank Susan
Robinson, Margaret Escombe, Belinda Rush-Jansen
and Celia Brooks-Brown for their valuable advice.

Thank you to Sadie Harrison for her inspiring musical
composition *With What do Summers' Winters Sing*.

CONTENTS

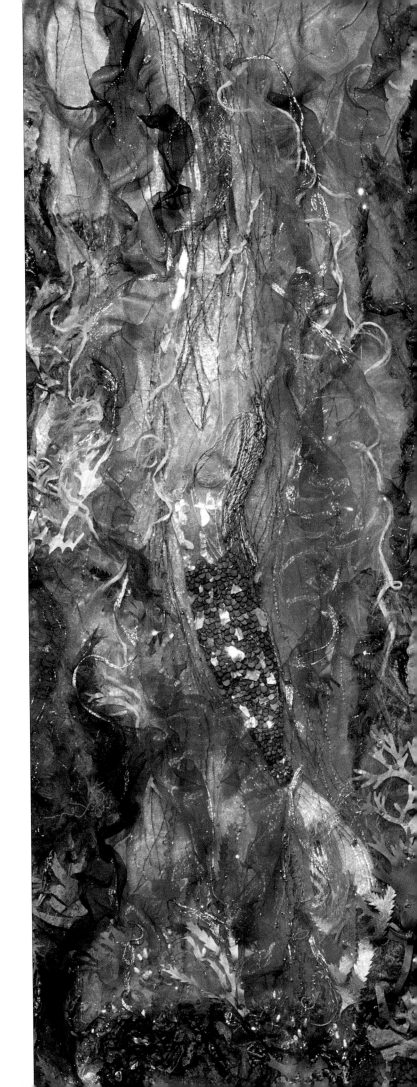

TO BEGIN WITH...

... what is now in my imagination was real to me. Foxgloves were quite simply that, gloves for foxes. Aquilegia flowers (fairies' bonnets) truly made the prettiest fairy bonnets, and pine needles were obviously meant to sew with.

Every living thing, every scuffling sound, every glinting light meant the world to me. I can remember countless hours exploring my world. People who did not understand, adults mainly, called it 'playtime' but it seemed to me far more important than that.

Playtime ... time to set tea for the fairies who hung their bonnets in the flower borders ... time to discover the paths that the fox had trodden in his gloved feet.

I would listen carefully to the sounds about me. The close sounds, the distant rustling, scuffling sounds. Insects buzzing and humming, birds singing and sending up alarm calls like bicycle bells. Strangely, I would rarely hear my mother call me in for tea.

I wrote letters to the birds (to keep in touch). Just simple notes enquiring after their health and asking them home for tea. I would post them into the garden hedge on the way to school along with a crumbled biscuit. They never came to tea but they always replied ... I listened very carefully.

I began my life as an artist during such playtime. It was where my imaginings began and I first sought the materials with which to explore them.

Daisies translated from nature into art (Daisies, page 100).

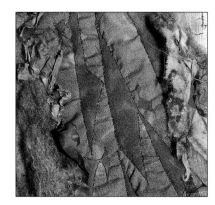

A corner of my studio, where treasured family heirlooms are gathered together with bottles, boxes and books containing things in which I delight. The four little drawers of the treasure chest in the background, delightfully papered with leaves, hold reels of vintage thread. Upon it rests a lichen-covered branch, referred to by the dear friend who gave it to me as 'wizard's beard'. The beautiful blue bottles which stand beside it were found close to home, buried by the many seasons which had passed since they were first abandoned there. A heart-shaped pin cushion brought home from the First World War by my great uncle rests amongst hand-embroidered braids, intricate lace collars and lacy handkerchiefs handed down to me by my grandparents. I cherish these things: their finery, their delicacy and the memories they evoke inform my creativity.

The texture of bark emulated in silk, cotton and hand-felted wool (Cloth of Bark, page 41).

INTRODUCTION

A dozen or so pebbles arranged in a picnic-rug square, acorn cups, oak-leaf saucers and petal plates weighted down with delicious morsels of snail shells and seeds, set neatly for fairy tea – one of my earliest memories of a creative childhood.

'Out of doors' was my favourite place to be; playtime 'in doors' only appealed on rainy days when fairy tea parties had to be postponed, when pine needles were too damp to 'sew' with and camps in the trees too bedraggled to be homely.

My love of the outdoors was encouraged by patient parents and grandparents, their own love of nature influencing my understanding and appreciation of it. Grandma and I would spend hours looking for tree-men in the knots and furrows of wood and making special expeditions to visit spots where we were sure that we had seen fairies. This love of the outdoors and fascination with the 'cloth of nature' has grown with me and now finds its expression in my work as a textile artist.

I studied at Loughborough College of Art and Design where I had excellent guidance from tutor Margaret Hall-Townley. She encouraged me to express the fascination with nature born of my childhood, to 'play' with fibres and stitches with no preconceived idea of technique. A personal understanding of textile media developed, and with it technique, not learned but natural and immediate to myself, enabling me to work intuitively.

I discovered fibres to be an exciting medium akin to the cloth of nature: woven and bonded cloth, spun threads, a multiplicity of fibre types all with different responses to stitch, dye and manipulation – a tremendous resource for artistic interpretation. I could create toadstools and stand them in fairy rings, stitch my grimacing little woodsmen, make them a tree, translate the fragility of a butterfly wing or the delicacy of a flower. I continue to discover new ways in which textiles respond, ways in which to interpret my ideas and bring my imagination to life.

I have over time refined my palette, now working largely in silk. Silk has the persuasion of petals and insect wings and a wonderful affinity with dye, enabling me to achieve nature's most startling colours and subtlest hues. I enjoy sparing use of synthetics for their translucency and for their texture when heat distorted. Interpreting reflective qualities often calls for snippets of metal-weave fabric and pure gold and silver threads. I also enjoy incorporating semi-precious stones, fragments of shell and iridescent feather.

My study is my artistic treasury. Picnic hampers holding fabrics are labelled from 'leaf greens' through to 'funny hues' and stacked high in the corners. Shoe boxes, cheese boxes and matchboxes with labels noting *beetles' backs*, *butterflies' wings*, *mermaids' scales* and other curious things are tucked away on shelves and inside drawers. Old printers' trays hold both things I have fashioned and those I have found: finished

butterflies' wings, silk petals and leaves with wires stitched carefully through their centres, a handful of ebony black bluebell seeds, the perfectly preserved velvety body of a bumblebee. Then there are the threads, the dyes and the things I use for sewing; the beads, the shells and the sparkly treasures. It is, in fact, organised chaos! There is a scientific theory that chaos is the natural order of things, in which case I have succeeded in bringing nature indoors, making it no longer second best to playing out of doors, or 'study in the field' as I euphemistically put it today.

I spend a great deal of time 'studying in the field', gathering resources for my work. I make jottings and sketches, take photographs and gather specimens of common flora. I have yet to bring an insect home against its will, though indulgent family and friends often bring me gifts of long-sleeping, dusty creatures retrieved from flower borders or behind curtains. I make frequent reference to natural history textbooks, finding myself fascinated by their elaboration of the smallest detail. Occasionally I will take a little sound recorder with me so that when I return to my studio I can listen in to the environment that inspires me: perhaps the sunny field where the white campion grows or the deep woods where the oak and beech leaves dance in the wind. Often I will make note of how my senses are affected, tracing my inspiration back to its core. I aspire to achieve works which are not simply observational but translations of wonder as well as nature.

Although I study the elements of my work carefully, accomplishing informative reference, I rarely make plans for a piece in its entirety. The strongest images of my finished work lie in my mind rather than on paper.

Dimension, space and freedom of movement are vital to nature and therefore inform my work, much of which is housed within deep box frames, its three-dimensional detail being carefully suspended, grounded or held inconspicuously on armatures or frames within the box frame. The works often comprise several layers, with one layer being glimpsed through another.

I work almost entirely by hand, slowly evolving each piece rather than bounding on towards the finish, adapting my ideas and changing my image of what this finish should be. I work for months, in rare instances even years, on a given piece, although my tendency is to evolve several pieces at a time.

As I have suggested I do not approach my work by way of technique, preferring to work intuitively, allowing the creative process to inform me. A stitch or fibre technique may be elaborately described in a textbook, but to me I have simply 'made it up' (although I humbly concede I have not!). I do find the unassuming stab stitch (even a non-conformist such as myself can readily identify that one!) of infinite value. Veining leaves, defining the pattern of a butterfly's wing or laying down the armour of a beetle – I find the simple rhythm of the stitch mesmeric.

Veil for Spring (detail)

It is invariably necessary to support the delicate elements of my work, from insects' wings to the tiniest of petals. I achieve this by stitching fine wires inconspicuously into place. Wires stitched beneath a butterfly's wing enable me to lift it into life. A hair-fine wire worked into the centre of a petal means that I can gently shape it to meet the centre of the flower, and the veins of a leaf, once wired, can be crumpled or twisted to hold its shape. With various weights of silk-bound wire I can interpret stems, roots, insects' legs and antennae … even the pine needles that I stitched with as a child.

An understanding of the inherent nature of my work does, however, lie before and beyond any methodology: in nature itself, in the eyes that see and the spirit that perceives. I look with wonder, and perceive a miracle; the pollen-dusted back of a bumblebee, the minute stamens of a flower, its delicate, radiating petals. I am in awe of what I discover. I believe that we are truly lost in the Garden of Eden. I hope that through my work I can encourage others to discover the paths that I have found, and the beauty that surrounds us all in the wonder of nature.

Jane E Hall

11

MATERIALS

The qualities of nature, from cobweb silk to clematis bine, from thistledown to the roots and crown of the winter aconite, command careful interpretation.

FABRICS

Silk is my best-loved fibre, spun by silkworms it is of pure, natural origin, therefore having an inherent affinity with nature. The lightest weights of habotai, chiffon and organza translate the most delicate of petals and leaves from nature into art. Silk satin emulates heavier, more sheeny petals and leaves like those of the snowdrop. Silk dupion, with its raw weft threads, perfectly suggests the veining of stronger plants like the winter aconite. Reflecting upon the beauty of a flower, the perfection of an insect's wing or, with my mind's eye, catching the glint and shimmer of a mermaid's tail or sensing the softness of an angel's wing, the subtle and seductive qualities of silk offer me limitless artistic possibilities.

I enjoy working with raw silk floss (silk tops; my working source of thistledown). Teasing out the fibres and gently blowing them across a flat surface, I bond them into a papery cloth from which I cut dragonfly, butterfly and bumblebee wings. This new cloth also yields beautifully to dyes.

Vintage reels of thread hold interpretations of snowdrops and wood anemones before they assume their place within finished pieces.

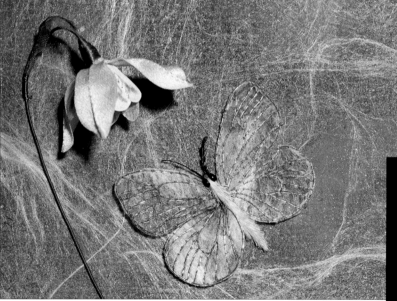

Snowdrop Illumination (detail)
A butterfly with wings of handmade silk paper rests beside a dainty snowdrop with painted silk satin and habotai petals. The mount they are against is covered with handmade paper and silk fibres.

A dandelion seed head, its feathery parachutes of seeds like thistledown, akin to the quality of silk floss.

A billowy cloud of undyed silks pulled from their storage baskets.

Papery cloth of bonded silk fibres from which I cut insects' wings.

13

DYED FABRICS

I largely work with fabrics in their natural, undyed state. Silk absorbs dye readily, retaining its lustre. Subtle shades and startling hues can be achieved by mixing and merging the dyes, working into the fabric in a loose and painterly style. I will often crumple the fabric as I work, allowing it to dry slowly; intense colour gathers in the folds and subtle shades disperse across the smoother expanses. It is often necessary to paint petals individually; barely touching a dye-tipped brush against their edges, each petal takes up its colour with a certain thirst.

These fabrics are collected into my artistic treasury together with lengths of shot silk, chiffon and organza, metallic weaves, iridescent sheer synthetics and fine bonded cloths. Together they are bundled into colour harmonies and stored away in wicker hampers, labelled descriptively under leaf and petal shades.

Asrai
A mermaid swims through a chiffon and organza sea, dancing with subtle weeds. They are cut from hand-painted silk in a multiplicity of weights, from the frothiest chiffon to the strongest dupion. Shimmering ribbons of crystal organza undulate amongst the weeds. Heat-distorted into bubbles, crystal organza further describes the mermaid's watery world. The mermaid is cut in silhouette from shell pink organza. Her tail is scaled with tiny pieces of silk, each the size of a pin head.

Wicker baskets full of harmonised fabrics.

Leaf Fall (detail)
*Leaves gathered from the woodland floor
are echoed here in lightweight silk, dyed
appropriately in mellow autumnal shades.
Wispy ribbons of transparent, watery blue
chiffon are floated across the surface of
the leaves and caught down with loose,
shimmery threads.*

15

NEEDLES & THREADS

Baskets and boxes contain my threads. Again, I favour silk. Lustrous silk floss, rainbow treasure, can be split into very fine strands and plied one with another to achieve an infinite variety of shades. Unplied they have even greater sheen, where nature calls for it. Perhaps the lobed green head of the snowdrop or the sun-lightened stems of tall grasses. By splitting down and twisting floss, one can achieve both delicate threads with which to work the finest detail and heavier threads for bolder expressions. I have also acquired vintage reels and skeins of flat and twisted silk, silk loom ends, braids and cords – generous gifts or table-top sale finds.

I have some beautiful vintage metallic threads with enchanting French labels, shimmery synthetic threads and pure gold threads from Japan. Thread with which to interpret every light in nature.

The needles with which I work are handmade, crafted with flat heads which do not bruise the delicate fabrics and threads that I use.

An intricately hand-carved needlecase.

A selection of silk and metallic threads organised into boxes in colour harmonies.

My desk, beneath the window for the best available natural light. Loose threads tumble out of a basket through which I search for the particular one I need.

I often draw my threads from the fabric with which I am working, making the stitches almost invisible. This is particularly the case where I am stitching to achieve form, as in the manipulation of shape into a petal, rather than to embellish or 'embroider' as in the detailing of a wing. Drawing perhaps as little as one petal's length at a time from my treasury, it seems to me a limitless resource.

A needlecase with four precious handmade needles caught into one of its pages; a length of pure gold and silk thread is wrapped around the other.

WIRE

Wire is an inherent element of my work. From its place at the centre of a petal or at the core of the tiniest silk-bound insect's leg, through to the proud stems of the water reed or the branches of an oak tree. I have weights finer than hair and thicker than willow and draw from my supply appropriately. I occasionally use fine wire decoratively, couching it into place as surface detail, perhaps in the veining of a butterfly's wing or the detailing of a fish's fin.

Here, the veining of the butterfly's wings is worked in fine copper wire, carefully stitched into place with fine silk thread.

An array of wires in various weights and colours suitable for different applications, from the centre of a petal to the branches of a tree.

CURIOUS DELIGHTS

Treasured away, I have tiny chips of semi-precious stone and fragments of shells, beads and seeds for insects' eyes, feathers for the patterning of their wings and many other curious things in which I delight. Whether or not they come to light in my work, they somehow nourish and inspire me.

A woodpecker's feather.

My study is my artistic treasury. Old printers' trays hold both things I have fashioned and those I have found. Beachcombings are collected into this tray. On the windowsill beyond, other finds are safely stored away in boxes and tiny drawers.

Seashells and pebbles inspire me with their iridescent colours, textures and that certain 'magic' that cannot be defined.

FRAMES

I support my work on a tambour frame or large, floor-standing frame, depending upon the scale of the work. Essentially, I create a working surface by stretching the frames with a sheer cloth against which I rest the piece I am stitching, ultimately, very carefully, cutting it free. Quite often and quite unconsciously the only support that I use is my hands.

Working on Dream Cloth, a large piece requiring the support of a floor-standing frame.

Dream Cloth (detail)
Here I am tracing the wing patterning of a fantastical moth in midnight blue shades of silk.

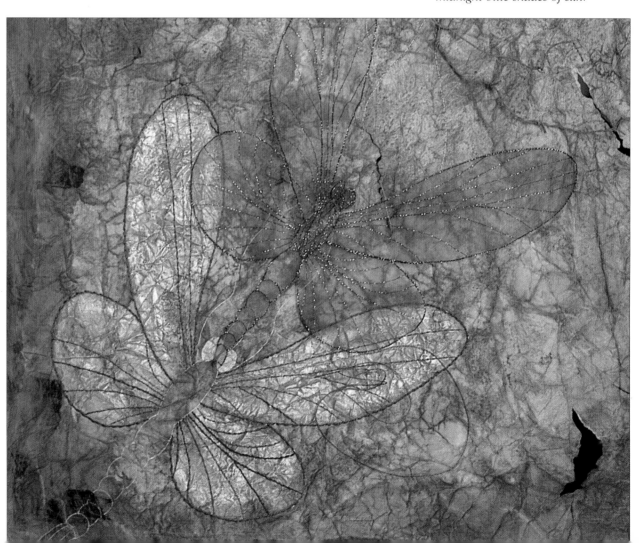

OTHER EQUIPMENT

The scissors that I use are very fine and very sharp, essential for the fine detail that I cut. My most curious tool is, perhaps, a flame – a tiny candle flame with which I seal and define the cut edges of fabrics, cut edges that I have not alternatively sealed with clear or metallic gutta (fabric dye, prescriptively used for outlining).

A magnifying glass can be a very useful tool with which to study and therefore better understand the detail in nature which I aspire to emulate.

My cedar workbox: pins, needles, bobbins, scissors, candles, matches and tailor's chalks are all found a place. Many more 'bits and pieces' lie beneath this sectioned tray and within other workboxes.

THE INSPIRATION

I draw the first breaths of inspiration for my artwork in the open air. Drawing close to nature I quietly watch and listen, meditate and merge with my environment. My senses honed, I work with the attitude of a naturalist, gathering impressions and information, essential references to take back to my studio where, through cross referencing, deliberating and reflecting, I go on to achieve an understanding of my subject conclusive enough by which to work.

When I am intent on information gathering, the invariable contents of my rucksack are sketchbook, notebook, soft pencil and sharpener, camera, tripod and an ample supply of film. Of course, there are many occasions when I wander off with no more than a biscuit in my pocket, still justifying these forays professionally as 'time in the field'.

In my studio I can carefully consider the inspiration that I have gathered 'in the field'. Here bottles of dye stand ready to be mixed appropriately to colour the leaves and petals of a particular plant. Beside them stand accomplished renditions snowdrops and wood anemones resting in vintage reels of thread.

The camera offers me greater immediacy, capturing light and environmental conditions as well as infinite detail. With a macro lens I can see into the secret world of nature, deep into the centre of a flower or into the crevices of a tree. I can come eye to eye with a rainbow beetle or watch the delicate tongue of a butterfly uncurl. With a telephoto lens I can see high up into the trees and draw far-away wonders nearer.

I am not intending to achieve perfect drawings when I am out and about, just simple sketches as memory aids, noting the colour, shape and scale of whatever treasure I have found. There are often more written lines in the margins than drawn lines on the pages of my field study sketchbooks. More accurate, careful renditions of my subjects are achieved in my studio.

Photographs help me to understand the subjects that inspire me.

A sketch and a silk painting observing snowdrops rest on my desk; progression towards the finished study Snowdrop Illumination (page 44).

MY STUDIO

More accurate, careful renditions of my subjects are achieved, when necessary to the piece they are informing, in my studio. There I have the appropriate paraphernalia, drawing boards, coloured pencils and the like, all far too cumbersome to trek out and about with.

Many of the drawings accomplished in my studio have a diagrammatical rather then aesthetic quality, particularly the plant studies. I carefully measure stem and petal length, the number of leaves, leaflets, petals, stamens, buds and seed heads so that, should its season pass whilst I am working a reflection of it, I retain a personal and certain knowledge of it. The minimum length of time that I have spent evolving a piece is two to three months, therefore it is invariably the case that any living reference I have been working with is, at best, faded or wizened by the conclusion of the piece.

*Here I am working on a sketch for Day Spring. Natural specimens lie side by side with
watercolour pencils, enabling me to make careful reference to colour and scale.*

*Sunlights spills in through the window, highlighting the work on my desk.
Close at hand are my sketchbooks and reference books, together with things
that inspire me: delicate seeds, soft feathers, lichens and little boxes full of
'hidden treasure'.*

NATURE'S TREASURES

Nature offers me treasures that I can bring home and study. I have an invaluable collection including shiny seeds, snail shells and seashells, perfectly preserved bumblebees, butterflies, a life-worn dragonfly and a papery dragonfly larva case. The list is growing with every new season that I explore. From childhood I have collected things – ladybirds in glass jars, tiny beetles in matchboxes, never wishing them harm, watching them scuttle away after an hour or two of play. As an adult, I stop short of butterfly nets, killing bottles and ether, collecting only what nature yields.

I collect things that I have found ... nature's treasures ... into old printers' trays. Placing seashell next to egg shell, fossil next to feather, coral next to lichen, I have built up rich, natural mosaics – inspirational resources for my work.

Old printers' trays hold things I have fashioned as well as those I have found. Mermaids' scales, the petals of a flower, leaves and silk-bound wire pine needles … many, many things, both accomplished and miniature works-in-progress. Eventually many will become incorporated into resolved works of art. Yet the printers' trays are like works of art in themselves; subtly, perpetually changing as new elements are introduced and existing ones find their ultimate resting place.

BUTTERFLIES

Nature's signature, butterflies, epitomise the beauty and miracle of nature.

My interpretations of these beautiful, delicate creatures often come to rest within one of my finished pieces, poised on leaves or flowers in the midst of the piece or resting, as if sunning their wings, at its margins.

My butterflies are born of my imagination rather than informed by entomological detail. I refer to size and shape but their 'essence' is imaginary. When I am asked about their origins, I often refer to them as extinct species! I once took great delight in making up nonsensical Latin-sounding names for a collective exhibit. Some visiting lepidopterists were overheard in disagreement as to whether or not they had seen certain of the species and, I might add, critical of my spelling!

Their wings are cut from papery silk-fibre cloth or hand-painted silk. Some are traced delicately with couched gold thread to suggest veining. Larger, more colourful butterflies, in the natural world referred to as 'the aristocrats', have bolder wings. These are achieved through layering contrasting silks or silk and feather, cutting a pattern from the top layer to reveal the layer beneath and then tracing around this pattern with a couched gold thread. It was observing the peacock butterfly which first inspired my use of peacock feather behind the cut-away silk. As, in nature's design, the eyes of a butterfly startle, the splendid iridescent colours of the feather are startling against the softer silk.

Their bodies are wire bound with a frayed silk ribbon; their eyes are tiny jet beads or shiny seeds and their antennae feather fronds. They are carefully under-wired, imparting strength and allowing me to gently manipulate them, lifting their wings into life.

A painted lady butterfly supping lavender nectar.

INSECTS

The beauty and variety of insect life is beguiling – beguiling me into artistic expression of my observations.

There are those which flourish their beauty – the butterflies, dragonflies and bumblebees – and those which play hide and seek – they hide, I seek. Beneath leaves, against petals, at the centre of closely cupped flowers, anywhere one is curious enough to seek them they are there to be found. There are those that use night time as their cover, commanding midnight forays. Moths, perfectly camouflaged by day, dance in splendid array in the moonlight from one sweetly night-scented nectar plant to another.

I have worked dragonflies, observing the fine tracery of their wings in gold and silk threads. I have worked beetles and bugs, tightly couching each shield of their armour separately, binding their tiny wire legs with feather fronds. I have worked lacewings and ladybirds, bumblebees and spiders, with each new insect making new observations and new artistic considerations.

My constant determination is not to copy, for one cannot copy a miracle, however tiny, but to honour.

It is believed that there may be up to two million
species of insect in the world, with new species
being discovered every year. Here are a few that I
have discovered in my imagination and described
through stitch.

FLOWERS & LEAVES

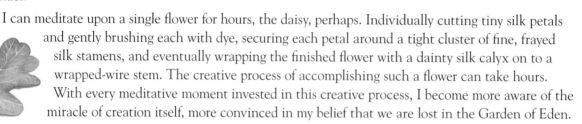

I t is with sheer wonder that I explore the life of flowers and leaves through my work, from counting the stamens at the centre of the daintiest flower, describing them in knotted silk floss or fine, frayed chiffon, through to cutting the boldest water reed from a heavy silk dupion. I live life as an artist, not simply to make beautiful things but, moreover, to better understand beautiful things. In describing what I see in fabric and thread, in staring into our natural world as an artist, I deepen my sense of wonder.

I can meditate upon a single flower for hours, the daisy, perhaps. Individually cutting tiny silk petals and gently brushing each with dye, securing each petal around a tight cluster of fine, frayed silk stamens, and eventually wrapping the finished flower with a dainty silk calyx on to a wrapped-wire stem. The creative process of accomplishing such a flower can take hours. With every meditative moment invested in this creative process, I become more aware of the miracle of creation itself, more convinced in my belief that we are lost in the Garden of Eden.

The basic techniques of cutting and piecing, surface stitching and invisibly stitching wire beneath details are quite easily understood in themselves; the difficulty lies in their application. Tiny pieces must be treated with great delicacy. A petal of fabric can be bruised or destroyed by a heavy hand, needle or thread. All three in combination lead to woeful consequences. A meditative yet determined mind, a gentle yet decisive touch are more valuable than any technical understanding.

Buttercup Reflection
(magnified detail)

35

FIGURES & FISH

I do not have to close my eyes to dream. The light of imagination projects angels and mermaids into my world, and fantasy in all its beauty flies and swims about me.

Using my resources as an artist I can make real the imagined. To catch a feather as it drifts, seemingly from nowhere, is to catch a glimpse of an angel. The feather has qualities akin to the silks with which I work. Moreover, the materials with which I work have qualities akin to my imagination. Thus my artwork evolves.

I perceive the glide of a mermaid's tail in a fold of silk and the lustre of her scales in tiny chips of seashell. Setting shell amidst tiny scales of silk I can play with light, subtly shifting colour and tone. So it is that I begin to realise a likeness of the mermaid who is so real to me in my imagination.

For each new piece that I work, whether its inspiration is drawn from the natural world or the realms of fantasy, I draw from the same 'language' to explain what I see – 'language' being the materials that I use and the techniques that I employ. As an artist I have found a voice with which to explain the beauty, the poetry and the fantasy that I perceive surrounds me.

Hope (detail)
The light of my imagination projects angels into my world, discovered in the shadows of secret places amidst the sway of branches or simply resting quietly at my shoulder.

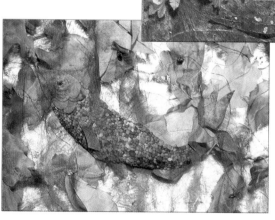

Leaf Fall (detail)
The shape and form imagination can take holds no bounds. In the orchestra of sound playing through our ancient woodlands, fish take shape, their scales glinting in the sunlight as they weave their course through the leaves.

A Thousand Finger Kisses (detail)
'She threw a thousand finger kisses towards the palace and swam upwards through the deep blue sea.'
(Hans Christian Andersen)

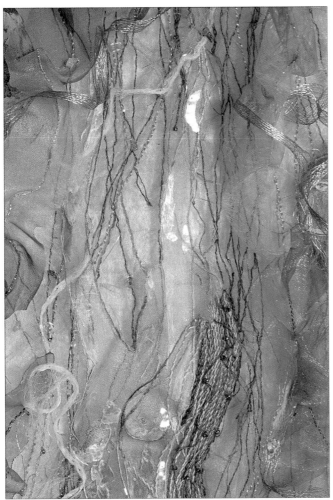

Asrai (details)
Her arms outstretched, a mermaid glides
gracefully through a silky blue sea.

Her tail is covered in tiny scales, each a fragment
of silk the size of a pin head, sealed and defined
with a candle flame. Tiny chips of ormer shell are
set amongst them.

Her tail brushes against the satin and organza
seaweeds of her embroidered world.

37

Cloth of Bark

The inspiration behind this piece is implicit in its title, *Cloth of Bark*. I imagined the bark of a tree to be the garment it wears. The silhouette of the piece was, however, informed by the shape of the tree rather than contrived to look like a dress. It was only as I completed the piece that I found I could wrap it around myself and strike a pose! As an artist, I am 'imagination-led' (occasionally misled!) rather than 'design-led'. Invariably I make no formal plans identifying a finished piece; my work evolves rather than resolving to a plan.

In defining the breadth of the base of the tree I found my hemline. The silhouette tapered gently from here towards a broad waist, and then, strong and true, it grew upwards towards the 'shoulders', the initial branches of the tree.

I ripped sections of paper and, holding them against the bark of the tree, rubbed across them gently with soft crayon, picking up an impression of the tree's texture. Placing these on my studio floor, echoing the tree's shape, dictated to me the method by which I would realise my 'cloth of bark'. By working textural panels of loosely felted wool and darker, heavier panels of rumpled and quilted cotton, and piecing them together, I began to realise the texture and form, the colour, light and shade of the tree. Piece by piece I could manipulate recessed areas and crevices; omitting panels entirely to echo a deep hollow at the base of the tree, I by chance fashioned a split to the knee!

In places where the felting was loose and sparse, I tugged out fibres across the space between panels, leaving sheer areas, further informing the light and shade of the piece. I created further texture by stitching fragments of silk, thread-bare cloth and heat-distorted organza across its surface.

Silk oak leaves and lichen further embellished my 'garment of the woods'. I then backed the whole patchwork of panels with a fine silk chiffon and over-stitched a wire behind the piece, outlining its shape and thus preventing it from draping and losing its silhouette.

The finished piece hangs from a polished branch gathered from the woods in which its inspiration grew. The piece would not be finished, however, without the tiny nest resting just below its hanging bough, or the moths resting against its surface.

Cloth of Bark
112 x 170cm (44 x 67in)
The silhouette of this piece is remarkably fashionable, with its nipped-in waist, strappy branches and flaring hemline. However, this was not contrived, but guided by careful observation of the tree's natural shape.

BARK

Photographs are an important part of my work. I use them to capture the colours and textures of nature, interpreting them in a spectrum of fabrics and threads. Intrigued by the patterns and shapes shown here, I recorded them so that I could use them later in my work.

A coloured pencil and watercolour sketch of a dark arches moth, spending its day with folded wings on a tree trunk, the cryptic colouring of its forewings making it almost invisible.

Photographs of bark, recording its colour and texture, helped to inform my choice of fabric and thread. Using them as reference, I collated different weights, colours and textures of materials from my textile artist's palette.

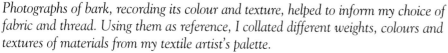

Using the photographs of different bark textures as reference, I decided upon the appropriate fabrics and threads for my 'cloth of bark'. Soft and sheer fabrics in earth tones harmonised with sheeny silk and heavier wool and cotton.

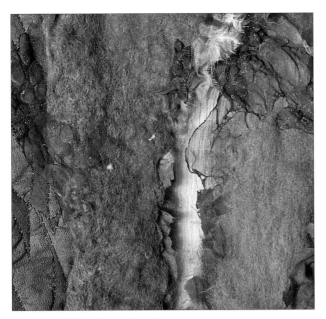

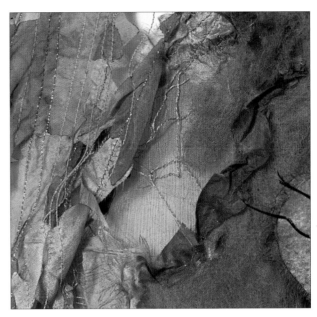

The felt panels are worked loosely from pre-dyed fleece in shades of mustard, brown and green. Working the panels separately, I could vary their weight, texture and hue and tease out their edges naturalistically. Piecing them together with frayed and torn silk and heat-distorted organza, I could manipulate crevices and knotty hollows into my emerging tree.

At the edges of the tree, towards its base, I ran stitches off the main patchworked fabric, catching in silk fragments to suggest tumbling leaves and leaf litter. This naturally softened the margins of the piece and further evoked an autumnal feel.

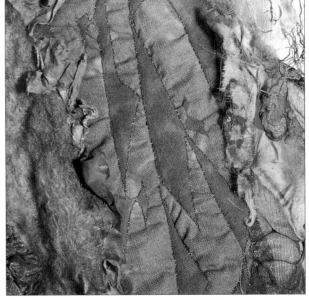

Lacy patches of threads worked over soluble fabric are pieced together with felt, quilted cotton, ripped silk scraps and fine bonded cloth. They are all backed with sheer silk chiffon which can be glimpsed through the lacy section. Silk habotai oak leaves are caught loosely across the surface, as if having tumbled from the tree.

The cotton panels are quilted with a black–bronze metallic thread. I manipulated the fabric as I worked, developing texture and creating gathers and dips for the dye to collect in, suggesting light and shade. The introduction of turquoise scraps of silk references a fungus called green wood-cup (Chlorosplenium aeruginascens) which mainly affects oak trees. The timber is used decoratively by cabinet makers and, I am sure, in many unknown fairy folklore traditions.

NESTS

I have spent many hours following pathless journeys into woods and thickets in search of nests, and many more into my imagination wondering where they might be and with what magic they are woven. Of course I have studied ornithologists' guides, watched nature documentaries and even been lucky enough to find two or three discarded nests, but my sense of mystery and enchantment remains undiscouraged by appraisal of factual information or sensible observation. Nests somehow surpass nature's purpose.

Crafting my own nests I can fully indulge my imagination and allow my sense of wonder in them to wallow. Many cup-shaped nests are begun in nature by her artisans, the hedgerow birds, with a foundation of spider's web. Lichen, moss, grass, hair, feather and down are then bedded in and woven carefully around the tiny bird's form, which as it twists and circles inside the growing nest forms the cup-shape fledgling home.

Unspun silk interprets cobweb well, spun plied silk emulates grass and hair. Frayed silk cloth suggests moss, and fabric snippets distorted with stitch suggest lichen. Twigs and branches can be conveyed with silk-covered wire. With patience and reverence for nature's true artisans, a nest, imaginatively speaking, comfortable enough to rest in after any flight of artistic fancy, can be formed.

Mysteriously, meticulously built, where people never think to look and rarely by happenstance find them, birds' nests perfectly quote the secret life of nature.

The cup-shaped nest, delicately woven and crafted, is held in position with a slender branch and tiny stitches.

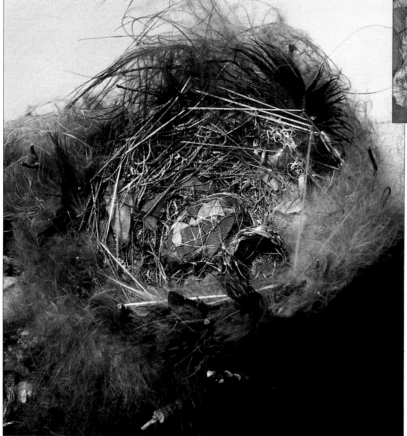

The nest is a delicate cup of threads, feathers and thistledown, woven and stitched together. Two tiny eggs, one broken, rest inside it. They are formed around acorns; a meticulous process of catching tiny fragments of silk across the acorn shell with a delicate needle and gold thread.

MOTHS

The moths rest, camouflaged against the bark of the tree, as they do in nature. They have wings of layered silk and feather, with their patterning cut away from the top layer of silk to reveal the contrasting silk and feather beneath. The patterning is traced around with a couched gold thread. Their bodies and legs are of frayed silk and feather; their eyes are semi-precious stones and their antennae feather fronds.

A coloured pencil sketch of a grey dagger moth found camouflaged against a tree.

A layered silk and feather moth, with hand-painted gold underwings, chips of tiger's eye for eyes and feather-frond antennae.

A moth of layered silk detailed with couched gold thread, with intricately cut gold and bronze underwings.

A moth with silk and feather forewings, hand-embroidered patterning and turquoise-chip eyes. Its frayed and tattered silk organza underwings are largely concealed.

Snowdrop Illumination

*Working sketch for
Snowdrop Illumination.*

There is such solace in a single snowdrop. The first flowers to forgive the hardship of winter, they coax the human spirit to relent of the despondency born of the cold, daylight-diminished days of December.

They tenaciously pierce the wintry earth with their vibrant green leaf blades. Flowering stems follow, protected by a sheathing bract or spathe. Opening, the moonlight-white flowers are redolent with the light and life of the springtime to follow.

The work of 'illuminators', the artist–calligraphers of ancient manuscripts and books of hours (books of prayer) has long inspired me. Naturalistic yet jewel-like illustrations of butterflies, insects, plants and foliage are set against borders surrounding a window which frames a further detailed painting illustrative of a bible story or another scene aiding devotion.

Snowdrop Illumination
*41 x 58cm (16 x 23in)
This 'illumination' honours
the snowdrop. Against a soft
green border covered with
wispy silk fibres lie delicate
snowdrops, a lacewing, a
butterfly and a beetle.*

SNOWDROPS

The snowdrops each have three silk satin sepals
and three green-tipped silk habotai petals with
very fine wire over-stitched through their centres.
They are gathered around a cluster of knotted silk threads
representing stamens. The stamens, petals and sepals are gathered
around a wire stem and bound into place using Japanese silk floss,
binding more intensely at the bulbous flower head, continuing
smoothly to the stem's base. A small, leaf-like, silk spathe is bound
into place to cover the tip of the flowering stem, emulating nature.
Green, silk leaf blades are wired to stand proudly within the piece
amongst the flowers.

*Accomplished snowdrops
arranged in a reel of vintage
thread before being stitched
into place within the piece.*

*A snowdrop lies against the
handmade paper and silk-covered
frame bordering the piece.*

The soft distance beyond the snowdrops photographed here is imparted to my snowdrop study by setting a mirror diffused with silk fibres at the back of the finished piece.

Snowdrops photographed against a rain-drenched windowpane.

Snowdrops rest gracefully in the window set amidst their proud, green leaves. A silk-diffused mirror beyond imparts a dreamy, reflective quality.

BORDER

The border surrounding the window is board covered in fine, hand-painted paper and wispy silk fibres. The silk fibres or 'tops' were teased out from their long, sleek skein and gently blown over the surface of the paper-covered board before being bonded into place. I then gently brushed across them with iridescent, silvery-white paint.

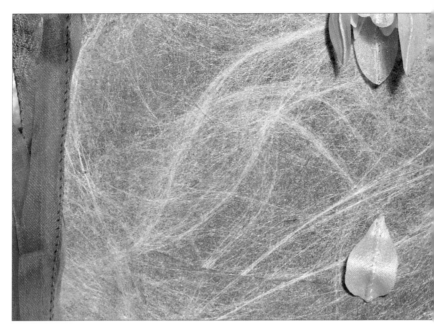

The lustre of the silk fibres swept across the border of the piece reflects the moonlight-white quality of the snowdrops.

LACEWING

There are understood to be forty-three species of lacewings in Britain ... perhaps now there are forty-four! This lacewing, a member of the 'silk species', suggests the nature of its inspiration rather than being a naturalistic copy. My aim as an artist is to emulate, not recreate. I humbly concede that the many and diverse qualities of nature in which I delight are imbued by God. I merely work with the materials and insight He grants the artist.

These delicate insects, with their translucent, lace-like wings, are often represented in my artwork. I use fine, bonded silk fibres for their wings which I trace with gold thread couched into place with tiny silk stitches. Their bodies are silk-bound feather quill, their legs silk-bound wire. For their eyes I use bluebell seeds which are in size and sheen akin to the insects' coal black eyes, which glow ember bright when caught in the light. Their long sensory antennae are represented with feather fronds.

BEETLE

The beetle, inspired by the flat, broad-bodied shield bug, is worked in couched gold thread. Each separate shield is like a miniature fingerprint traced around with gold thread, couched into place using fine silk threads. Each of the shields is then in turn stitched to a soft bodyform made from fine bonded cloth and silk wadding. His diminutive legs are feather-bound wire, his eyes are seeds and his antennae feather fronds.

My rendition of a shield bug, at just 2cm (¾in) wide, the size of my fingerprint.

BUTTERFLY

The butterfly has delicate, semi-translucent wings of bonded silk fibres. Their patterning is traced in gold thread caught into place with tiny silk stitches. Its body is frayed silk; it has two jet black eyes and feather antennae. Finally, the wings are invisibly wired and lifted into life.

Green shield bug (Palomena prasina).

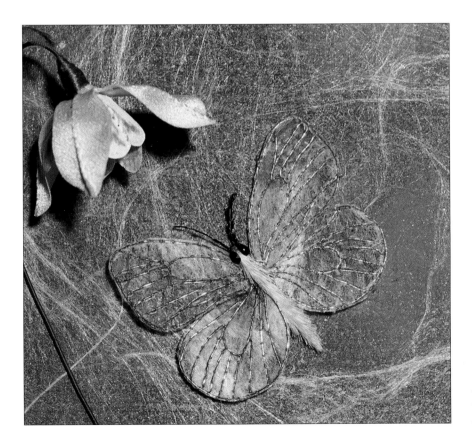

A butterfly with a dainty wingspan of 4cm (1½in) rests against the border of the piece.

49

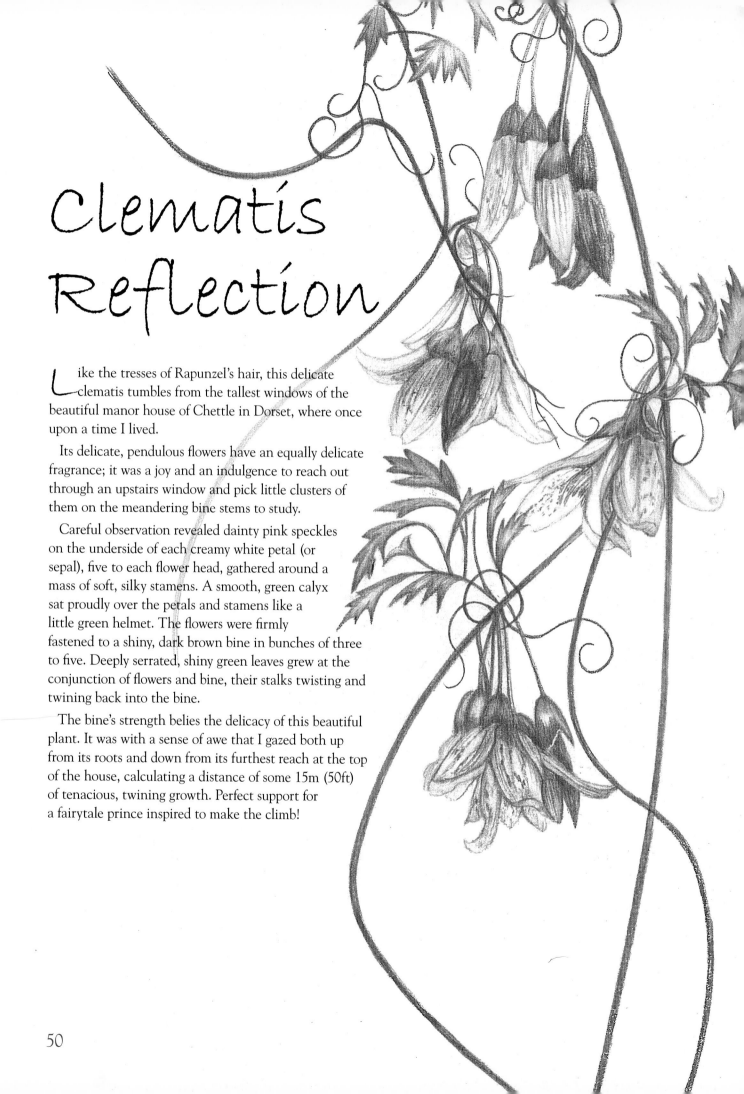

Clematis Reflection

Like the tresses of Rapunzel's hair, this delicate clematis tumbles from the tallest windows of the beautiful manor house of Chettle in Dorset, where once upon a time I lived.

Its delicate, pendulous flowers have an equally delicate fragrance; it was a joy and an indulgence to reach out through an upstairs window and pick little clusters of them on the meandering bine stems to study.

Careful observation revealed dainty pink speckles on the underside of each creamy white petal (or sepal), five to each flower head, gathered around a mass of soft, silky stamens. A smooth, green calyx sat proudly over the petals and stamens like a little green helmet. The flowers were firmly fastened to a shiny, dark brown bine in bunches of three to five. Deeply serrated, shiny green leaves grew at the conjunction of flowers and bine, their stalks twisting and twining back into the bine.

The bine's strength belies the delicacy of this beautiful plant. It was with a sense of awe that I gazed both up from its roots and down from its furthest reach at the top of the house, calculating a distance of some 15m (50ft) of tenacious, twining growth. Perfect support for a fairytale prince inspired to make the climb!

Clematis Reflection
30 x 58cm (12 x 23in)
A study of clematis
(Cirrhosa var
balearica).
*A delicate yet
tenacious plant
making the heady
climb of some 15m
(50ft) against a wall
of Chettle Manor
House, Dorset.*

51

BINE

Informed by careful observation, I began my clematis study. My initial consideration was the bine itself, representing its growth and movement throughout the piece. I began by echoing it in the distance of the composition with long, swaying runs of silk stitches and brush-painted lines on to sheer silk organza. I then painted in the curling bine tendrils, clusters of flowers and leaves. I repeated this process on to a second panel of sheer silk organza and over-laying one with the other I began to create an illusion of depth.

Working on the principal panel of the piece, leaving the second subtly detailed and diffused beneath, I brought the strength of the bine forward, representing it with silk-bound wire. At intervals I bound in loose, twisting threads to represent its tendrils.

Through the window of my studio, a different species of climbing plant can be glimpsed … inspiration, perhaps, for a future study.

Having attached lengths of this bine in twisting patterns across the piece I stitched cut silk leaves on to the bine and against the painted background. Wired through their mid-veins I was able to manipulate them forward to rest naturalistically within the composition. I then attached the pendulous flower heads to the bine and backdrop with long, green, silk stems.

The flower buds were formed by gathering silk up into a point and cupping it inside a piece of green silk stitched into the form of a calyx. Painted silk habotai and knotted silk stamens were similarly stitched into a tiny cupped silk calyx to represent the open clematis flowers.

The delicate, pendulous flowers of the clematis, translated here into silk, each separate petal carefully hand painted.

BUTTERFLY

I worked pale green and silver threads over soluble fabric to create the lacy cloth surrounding the piece against which a delicate butterfly rests. The butterfly has painted silk habotai wings, their patterning traced with a couched gold thread.

I used fine pure gold and silk thread to trace the delicate patterning on to the wings of this 'clematis butterfly'. Stitching a fine wire beneath the wings enabled me to lift them naturalistically into life, away from the surface of the piece.

Sea Pink

The sea pink, or thrift, so named after its ability to thrive on rugged cliff tops and the infertile terrain of salt marshes, is perhaps the most prolific flower of our coastline. With deep, woody roots it anchors itself into cracks and crevices forming cushions of soft, spiny leaves which flourish with pink blossom from May until August.

They are blowsy like the blush of an intrepid walker, undaunted by the buffeting winds and salty sea spray. They survive the thirsty summer months tapping water from a constant supply deep below the surface terrain, and lose little through evaporation from their fine, needle-like leaves.

Perhaps it is an association endeared by their habit of closely hugging the earth (which in truth prevents the plant roots from drying out) which draws its age-old association with 'sympathy', but I fancy that it is more likely its soft, pink, graceful presence, so sympathetic to weary walkers such as me. Indeed they also engender the sense of elation that one feels upon reaching the cliff top and gazing out into the magnificence of the sea.

Exploring the shoreline, Durdle Door, Dorset.

Inspired by the Jersey thrift, I began this piece in a painterly fashion, softly sponging and stippling dyes on to a pale blue, silk backcloth. I then over-layered chiffon and organza, floating them across the piece and catching them down gently with minute stitches. To achieve denser effects within the composition, suggesting the cliffs and rocky terrain of the foreground, I folded and manipulated the fabrics as I worked.

I defined the piece further with silk stem stitch and the application of thin, dark green leaves cut from silk dupion and sealed and defined at their edges with a candle flame. The flower heads in the mid-distance are clustered fragments of silk, cut silk petals and tiny chips of semi-precious stone. The three-dimensional flowers in the foreground were achieved by pinching cut silk petals together and securing them on to a stem of silk-bound wire with fine stitches. The whole composition, once resolved, was diffused further, as if by a soft sea mist, with chiffon made thread-bare by withdrawing many of the warp and weft threads.

The picture mount representing the sea is of dyed silk fibres and chiffon over painted board. Thrift flowers are caught in the chiffon folds as if caught in the waves of the sea.

Sea Pink

60 x 60cm (24 x 24in)

A beautiful wave of sea pink billows against the Jersey coast. It is as if a magical, exuberant tide has brought it from far away where the ocean is deep; where rainbows sink and mermaids colourwash their tails.

BACKGROUND

The soft, hazy colour and light of the cliff tops is captured here in the subtle layering of chiffon over fabric dyes, applied in a painterly, impressionistic style. The layers are denser in the distance, representing the deep, restless sea and craggy cliff line. I have further defined the cliff line by sharply folding the layers of chiffon to create ridges.

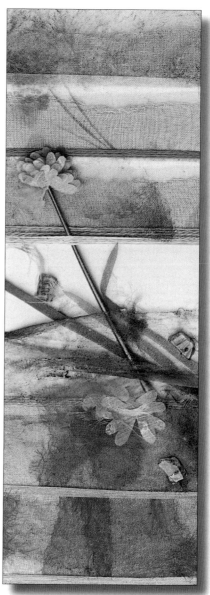

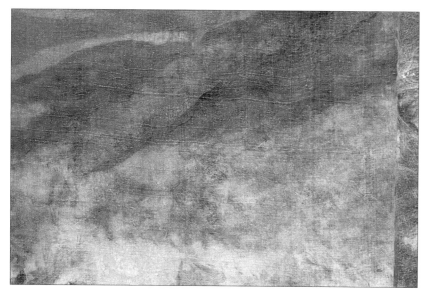

Through the subtle layers of chiffon, soft pinks and blues merging into mauve, you can glimpse the impressionistic painting of sea pinks.

The thrift flowers in the mid-distance of the piece were initially painted on to the backcloth in a loose, impressionistic style in subtly differing shades of pink. They were then over-laid with snippets of chiffon and cut silk petals and embellished with chips of rose quartz and tourmaline, reflecting any light falling on the piece. Fine, needle-like leaves were cut from silk chiffon and stitched amongst the flowers. Further leaves are detailed with silk stem stitch.

Sea Pink fabric and thread swatch, essential reference to my palette of materials as I am working.

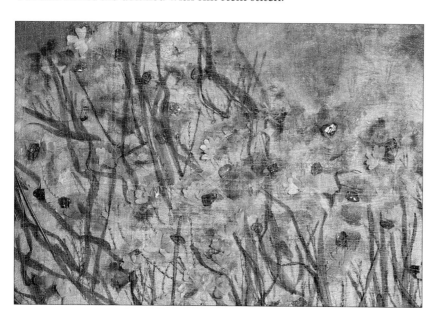

In the mid-distance the work becomes slightly less impressionistic. The thrift flowers are more defined, cut petals and chips of rose quartz are stitched against the painted backcloth, standing in light relief.

FLOWERS

The thrift flowers in the foreground spilling on to the mount in the corner of the frame were worked three-dimensionally. Tiny silk petals were cut from hand-painted silk habotai and pinched and stitched together on to silk-bound stems. They are set amidst leaves cut from various weights of silk, from chiffon to dupion, expressing depth within their habitat.

Several flowers tumble away from the central image to be caught into the mount as if drifting in the surf, suggested by the chiffon with which it is covered.

The flowers spilling across the mount in the corner of the study are worked three-dimensionally. Tiny cut silk petals are grouped in dense flower heads on to silk-bound wire stems.

FRAME

The mount is board, wrapped in silk fibres and painted to echo the colour, light and shade of the sea. It is then covered with fine chiffon caught down into waves and folds to suggest the movement of the sea, its foam and surf.

Thrift flowers seemingly bob in the chiffon surf bordering the piece.

Falling Leaves

My very first needle was almost certainly 'pine'. More like pins than needles, pine needles were invaluable for sewing leaves one to another and making canopies. Canopies to hang in the trees, to drape over the washing line and dance beneath, or perhaps to rest softly on the lawn as a picnic blanket to gather fairies or song birds around for tea.

The leaves in this piece (which I'll admit to having draped across my shoulders) were cut from fine silk chiffon and organza. Their edges were sealed and defined with a candle flame, or painted with gold gutta (fabric paint). Some were splattered and sponged with gold gutta to reflect the glinting light of nature. Pine needles – pieces of fine wire bound first with a raw silk thread and then with a finer, sheeny, dark silk thread – attach the leaves to each other. Up to five single knotted stitches secure each one in place. Much to my dismay, silk and wire do not hang together as well as the 'real thing'!

The butterfly was created from two layers of silk; one chiffon, one hand-painted habotai. The top layer was cut away, using scissors with tiny points, to reveal the sheer layer beneath; this patterning is then traced around using gold thread couched into place with tiny stab stitches. Its body is frayed silk, its eyes are glass beads and antennae feather fronds.

Falling Leaves
26 x 94cm (10 x 37in)

The autumnal splendour of the copper beech, Chettle Park, Dorset.

LEAVES

Having gathered fallen oak leaves from the woodland floor I traced their shapes on to fine silk chiffon and organza. Carefully cutting them out, I dropped them to fall in a new pattern on my desk. Taking pine needles – silk-bound wire imitating nature – I began fixing one leaf to another, leaf by leaf, creating a canopy akin to those I had made as a child. Each pine needle was secured using a 'real' needle with single knotted stitches. At times I believe I have, to an extent, avoided having to 'grow up' by simply adapting the things with which I play!

Fallen leaves gathered on the woodland floor.

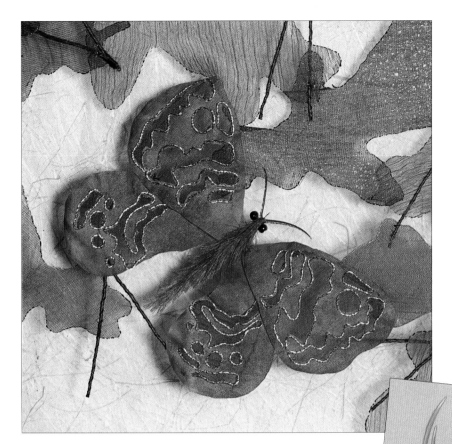

BUTTERFLY

A butterfly dances amidst the falling leaves, its delicate, hand-painted silk wings touching and joining the tumbling pattern. Its layered silk wings are in part the chiffon of the oak leaves, unifying it with the piece. Fine gold thread couched into place with tiny silk stitches traces the cut-away patterning of the wings. Its bright eyes are tiny glass beads, its soft, silken body frayed silk.

Watercolour pencil sketch. A primrose flourishes from the woodland floor. The fallen leaves of many seasons past sustain new life.

Pastel and pencil sketch of pine cones.

sunshine

The sunshine-yellow flowers of the winter aconite beam brightly from the wintry woodland floor. Radiant like a smile, they light up the new year. Aconites are the first yellow flowers of the new year, opening their shiny sepals as the strengthening light of early spring alights and warms them. They flower resplendently into March as if, by their virtue, drawing the full flourish of spring forward.

Tucked inside radiating crowns of sepals, they hide tubular petals holding droplets of nectar to coax and delight insects, rare this early in the year. Each flower is surrounded by a ruff of leaf-like, deep green, glossy bracts, protecting the buds before they open. The aconite's true leaves remain beneath the earth until the flowers have withered when they emerge, highly toxic, to protect the plant.

I began my study of the winter aconite by knotting a web of sheeny Japanese silk floss across a pierced Perspex frame, catching in chips of amber and citrine as I worked. My intention was to spin a web of light to support the whole piece by originating the work in a sense of sunshine with radiating, shimmering threads and sparkling semi-precious stones.

I then echoed the shape of the leaf bracts, themselves like miniature sunbursts. I cut them from hand-painted habotai, chiffon and tussah silk, singeing their cut edges with a candle flame to seal and define them. I then scattered them across my 'web of sunshine' catching them carefully into place with single knotted stitches.

Undulating across the canopy of leafy green and gold aconites, I stitched lengths of mossy green, frayed silk over-stitched on to fine wire, emulating the mossy green habitat of the aconite. The whole piece is bordered by a dark green, frayed silk ribbon and housed in a deep, mirrored box frame diffused with shot gold organza.

Finally, three butterflies were brought to rest within the piece. In nature, butterflies would be rare indeed amidst such early spring flowers, but in the secret sunlight of a hidden woodland hollow where no human eye may glance, they may yet rest.

Throughout my work my renditions of these beautiful creatures are never an attempt towards realism, more they are flights of artistic fancy. I consider their qualities, their patterning and iridescent colours, their delicate bodies and dainty antennae. I reflect, then venerate not recreate. Their true beauty, born of heaven, barely approached by any artistic endeavour that I may make.

The radiance of winter-flowering aconites, from their beaming, sunshine-yellow flowers and radiating sepals through to the way in which they light up the woodland floor, inspired this study.

Sunshine

44 x 90cm (17 x 35in)
The sunshine-yellow flowers of the
winter aconite inspired this study
of the woodland floor. A carpet
of silk-petalled flowers with bright
amber and citrine centres and
deeply serrated leaves (or bracts),
themselves like miniature sunbursts,
suspended on a sheeny, floss silk
web over a bright mirror covered
with shot organza.

BUTTERFLIES

The butterflies have hand-painted silk wings intricately cut away to reveal iridescent feathers held beneath with another layer of fine fabric. The cut-away patterning is then traced around with a fine gold thread couched into place with tiny silk stitches – this detailing also catches together the layers of each wing. The wings are then wired inconspicuously giving them extra strength and life before being attached to delicate, frayed, silk-bound bodies with jet black seed beads for eyes and feather-frond antennae.

One of three butterflies sunning its silken wings amidst the aconites.

The eyes of iridescent colour on this butterfly's wings are peacock feathers layered beneath the cut-away surface layer of the wings. They are traced around with a gold thread carefully couched into place with tiny silk stitches.

Swatch of Sunshine fabrics and threads.

In this detail you can clearly see the tiny chips of amber and citrine caught into the web on which the butterfly rests and the frayed, silk-covered wire undulating across its surface offering a mossy quality to the piece.

BACKGROUND

In the very distance of the piece the shimmer of crystal organza against the mirror imparts the sparkling light of sunshine. The faint shadows of the aconite flowers and bracts, and the silken hammock upon which they rest, are cast by the sun shining on to the piece.

A sheeny web of floss threads worked across a pierced Perspex frame created a hammock upon which to rest the aconites and silken-winged butterflies.

Leaf Fall

The once silky mists of early autumn now hang heavy and cold in the air, dampening the day's light. It is late morning before the sun is strong enough to kindle the embers of an autumn, now fading into winter.

The colour still dancing in the trees is called eagerly to blanket the earth. Nipped by early frosts and buffeted by keen winds, it tumbles leaf by leaf to the woodland floor.

Fallen leaves deepen into drifts which, from childhood, have called me out to play, to strike them back into the air with my boot, to gather armfuls and cast them back into the wind and dance with them as once again they fall back down to earth. Their sound, their scuffling, rustling, bustling sound, has always delighted me. As a child, when I heard an autumn wind buffeting through the trees and fallen leaves, it convinced me that I was on the shore of a great sea. As the sound fell, it fell like water breaking over rocks, as it played more softly it was like the murmur of a brook or the trickle of a stream. On family walks, as we trudged on seemingly endlessly with little time to stop and play, I remained convinced that we would eventually reach the water's edge. I imagined the fun I would have, mindful, of course, of the parental adage, 'as soon as you get wet, Jane, we will have to go straight home.'

Leaf Fall is an expression of this perception of sound, this altered sense of reality which still abides with me today, though now I am no longer eager to meet the water's edge, simply content to bathe my senses in the light, colour and sound which surrounds me. Fish with tiny silk scales, individually stitched into place using a fine warp thread of the fabric from which they were cut, swim through leaves, stitched where they touch using single knotted stitches. As with all my work, the majority of the fabrics and threads used are hand dyed with colour- and light-fast dyes used in a painterly fashion. With the exception of one run of machine stitches, the piece is worked entirely by hand.

The water's edge, Durdle Door, Dorset.

Leaf Fall

68 x 99cm (27 x 39in)

*Inspired by the ocean of sound played through the trees by a lively wind, I
conceived of this piece. Leaves form a wave and fish swim sinuously from
my imagination to weave their way through them.*

LEAVES

Oak, beech, maple and hawthorn leaves gathered from drifts on the woodland floor are echoed here in lightweight silk, dyed appropriately in mellow autumn shades. Wiring many of them through their mid-veins enabled me to express movement within the piece, lifting and twisting them as if buffeted by the wind as I stitched them into place. They are caught together invisibly with individually knotted stitches. Wispy ribbons of transparent, watery blue chiffon are floated across the surface of the leaves and caught down with loose, shimmery threads, conveying the imagined flow of water and strengthening the whole structure of the piece. Chips of semi-precious stone caught in with the chiffon ribbons glint in the light as sun sparkles over water.

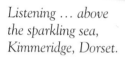

Listening … above the sparkling sea, Kimmeridge, Dorset.

Deeper into the woods I tread as if wading out to sea. Beneath my feet leaves break and drift, above my head they stir and tumble. Sound ebbs and flows like the tide. Then, at once, the air is as rushing water. Boughs wave, leaves ride upon them, some so buffeted they dive and dance to earth, a fall of colour and light. A play of sound, percussive tapping, tickling leaf fall like waterfall, falling to a whisper. Quiet laps my senses, sunlight swims and sinks about me. A sea of calm overwhelms me.

Swatch of fabrics and threads used in Leaf Fall.

Many of the leaves are wired, a fine copper wire being stitched into place along their mid-veins, enabling movement to be manipulated into the piece. Wispy ribbons of chiffon from which the piece hangs float across the work, strengthening its structure. They are loosely stitched with iridescent threads, knotted at intervals with chips of semi-precious stone.

FISH

Fish swim the enchanted sea of sound high up in the trees and dabble in the shallow leafy streams beneath the feet of walkers with imagination.

Three fish swim against a restless tide of leaves. Their bodies are cut from hand-painted, lightweight silk, their gills, fins and tails are cut separately, over-layered and stitched into place. Their eyes are detailed with gold thread, couched down with tiny silk stitches. Their bodies are covered in miniature silk scales. Each separate scale is sealed and defined around its edge with a candle flame and carefully stab stitched into place using a very fine needle and very fine thread in order not to bruise and destroy it. The whole process commands great patience and grace, being delicate and slow to accomplish.

Measuring 15cm (6in) from tip to tail this fish's scales are just 2mm ($^1/_8$in), each caught down with a tiny silk stitch.

Fish set amidst a sea of wispy silk chiffon and drifting leaves.

Beneath a smuggler's cave, Durdle Door, Dorset. I rest contentedly on a seat hollowed into the rock by countless tides. With sketchbook and pencil I could meditate here for hours.

In the presence of the sea, walking the silky sands of the shore, dabbling my toes in the foamy surf or, high up, exploring the cliff tops, I am blissfully content. I dabble my imagination in the deep turquoise shadows of the sea, glimpsing mermaids and sea angels. In the echoing, billowing, gargling sounds of the deep I hear the shuffling of these otherwise silent, imaginary creatures as they come ashore.

I am in awe of the natural beauty that abounds – the miniature creatures often identified only by their miraculous shells; the plant life of the sea and of the coastline. Beyond the sea I look to the sky where magnificent creatures take to the wing, and where mares' tails in the cloud become unicorns' tails, and once again my imagination canters and gallops.

Hope

I am in the grounds of the Wintershall Estate, in the audience of the
Wintershall Passion Play. About me, eucalyptus trees tower into the
brightest blue sky like the buttresses of a vaulted ceiling. Eucalyptus leaves,
fallen and crushed in my path, usher a heady scent, like incense. I gather a
handful – long, delicate and pointed like feathers – and fan them out in my
palm. I find I am holding an angel's wing.

A passage from my diary quotes the inspiration for this piece. I had spent
the day following actors playing out the life of Christ in the beautiful grounds
of the Wintershall Estate in Surrey: Scene by scene they moved the setting
– beside the stable, the lakeside, beneath the trees – carrying our conviction
for the story they told with them, weaving us into its very fabric. Actors who
embodied their characters so eloquently moved amongst us, sat and stood
beside us, causing us to believe that we were living the story rather than
watching it. My imagination was rendered sensitive to delicate imagery and
this angel was projected by the light of the whole experience against my
mind's eye.

I sketched the figure of the angel into my diary and carefully tucked the
leaves (or feathers as they seemed to me) of her wing between its pages to
contemplate her later in my studio.

In fact, my first consideration was to find my angel, who I named Hope,
somewhere to rest. Inspired by the tall, arching branches of the eucalyptus
trees, I cut an arched window from fibreboard and commenced to cover it
with silk fibres and pressed eucalyptus leaves, painting them with olive, grey,
copper, bronze and gold metal powders, slowly building up a rich, textured
frame within which she could be set. I stretched two layers of semi-translucent
chiffon across the window, having painted them irregularly with pale bronze,
gold and copper fabric paints, allowing them to crinkle and peel as they
dried, rendering a certain delicacy and fragility to the backdrop for my angel.
Echoing the shape of a eucalyptus leaf, long, delicate and pointed, I stitched a
feather against this surface as if it were softly falling to rest, using various floss
and hand-plied silk threads.

Two lacewings also rest on the borders of the piece, their wings veined with
pure gold thread couched down with silk stitches, their bodies and tiny legs
bound in the same lustrous gold.

Finally, a mirror is set at the back of the piece illuminating it from within as
it catches the light.

Hope
43 x 92cm (17 x 36in)
For Jemma.
A gentle angel alights the sill of an arched window. She pauses, resting her soft, silk feathered wings.

A peacock's
breast feather.

Storyboard exploring the information gathered
to inspire the piece and the materials used.

The arched window
whose shape is echoed in
the window against which
the angel rests.

I was inspired to work this piece whilst sitting
beneath towering eucalyptus trees in the
grounds of the Wintershall Estate.

ANGEL

"'Hope' is the thing with feathers
That perches in the soul
And sings the tune without the words
And never stops – at all"

From a poem by Emily Dickinson, 1830–1886.

My angel, Hope, is detailed in dark brown silk thread with wisps of bronze, gold and brown silk hair tumbling across her shoulders. Her wing, initially cut in silhouette from gold silk organza, is covered with silk feathers, individually cut from frayed silk ribbons before being carefully stitched into place. Downy fronds of real feather gathered from the grounds of the Wintershall Estate rest on her shoulders, stitched there securely and invisibly.

Swatch of fabrics and threads used to evolve the piece.

FEATHER

This delicate feather is stitched in subtle shades of soft terracotta and white. The threads are hand-plied to achieve this delicate harmony. Some are worked unplied or 'flat', imparting a sheeny quality. Its shape echoes that of the eucalyptus leaves which inspired the form of the angel's wing.

A soft, downy owl's feather.

LACEWING

During the spring and summer I have observed that lacewings sparkle green. As the year progresses, they adopt the soft bronze camouflage of this creature, more appropriate to the autumn scene. With its wings held across its back, it stands on six diminutive legs made from fine wire bound in gold thread. Its body is similarly constructed with wire and thread. Its wings are embroidered with heavier gold thread couched down with tiny, dark bronze stitches.

A lacewing rests camouflaged against a border of collaged silk fibres and eucalyptus leaves, richly burnished with gold and copper metal powders and dappled with iridescent silver paint.

BACKGROUND

Silk organza eucalyptus leaves tumble down the frame and across the window. Many are embroidered with gold thread, tracing the pattern of their veining, couched into place with tiny stab stitches. They all had wire stitched through their mid-veins, enabling me to manipulate them naturalistically as I stitched them into place.

This detail illustrates the gothic curve of the window and the elegant pointed leaves of the eucalyptus, cut from hand-painted silk organza.

Asrai

Rock pooling … one might find furbelows and dabberlocks, peacocks' tails and red rags, sea anemones and limpets, sea mice and cat worms! Rock pools are like little, warm cauldrons into which the sea has cast salty spells.

Far away, where the sky meets the sea and it glistens brimful of stars, there in the fathomless deep, mermaids dwell.

As the moon draws the tide they dance with its flow. Like kite ribbons on a zephyr, they drift through the vast deep. Gracefully they climb, the light of every sunset, every dawn, mirrored in their scales. Their furthest reach, beyond the sea, their heaven, where on crests and waves their world billows into the sky; where feathered spirits soar into the blue beyond; where the sea becomes a symphony and they rejoice, reborn to hear; where they can feel the sun, and sing hymns to its dawn and its setting. Dispersing like a spell in the sight of man.

I once met a lady who captured my imagination in speaking of her husband fishing the Jersey sea for ormer shells, primarily for the delicacy inside. My fascination was not culinary however, but found in the magical, pearlescent shells themselves. Weeks later I received a parcel, inside which there was a clutch of ormer shells. I crushed one, and the fragments were like tiny scales; tiny scales which became the shimmer in this mermaid's tail.

Flotsam and jetsam, ropes and floats, are woven into a mermaid's tail by a restless sea and washed ashore.

Asrai

40 x 76cm (16 x 30in)
A mermaid swims through a sea, dancing with subtle weeds, sparkling with light. Imagery conveyed using silk and crystal organza, semi-precious stone and pearlescent shell.

A storyboard exploring my inspiration for Asrai.

A swatch of fabrics and threads used to express my inspiration.

MERMAID

Asrai's body is outlined and subtly detailed with seashell-pink silk thread. Fragments of translucent shell are then stitched against her body accentuating its curves and form. Her hair is twists and wisps of silk and pure gold, tightly stitched to swim against her form.

Ormer shells, oreille de mer, *from the Jersey coast and a pearlescent top shell.*

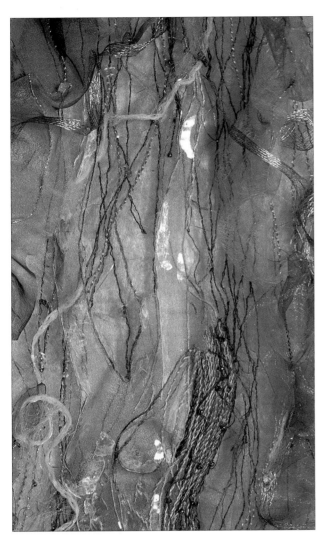

The mermaid is depicted with her arms outstretched rising gracefully through a silky sea dancing with ribbons of shimmering fabric and delicate, hand-cut weeds. She is cut in silhouette from shell-pink organza brushed with iridescent dye. She is detailed in outline with couched silk thread; the fragmented shell highlighting her curves is minutely drilled before being stitched into place.

Her tail is made up of tiny fragments of silk singed individually at their edges with a candle flame, with the ormer shell set amongst them. They are stitched one by one on to a ground of painted silk cut into the mermaid's shape.

81

The tail fins of the mermaid are painted in shades of seashell pink and embroidered with silk and gold threads couched into place with fine silk stitches. Silk seaweeds cut with very fine scissors and caught with chips of crystal brush against her tail as it fans through them.

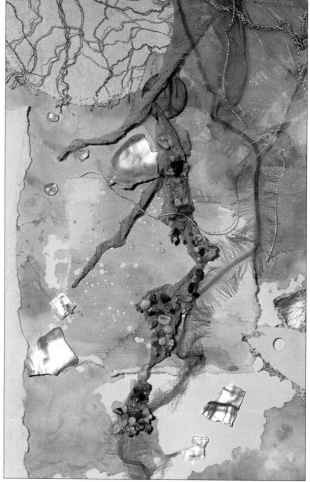

A corner of the storyboard exploring my inspiration for Asrai. Here chips of semi-precious stone, tails of silk chiffon and frayed silk ribbons express the qualities of the sea through which the mermaid swims.

BACKGROUND

The mermaid is caught on to a sheer, wispy, blue cloth with long, wavy runs of stitches in muted ocean shades. Many of these runs of stitches are then whip stitched with further silk threads and caught with silver beads, pearls and chips of semi-precious stone which catch any light reflected into the piece.

Silk threads knotted with silver beads, suggestive of bubbles, hang freely away from the piece. Seaweed cut from hand-painted silk is caught invisibly into place as if drifting through its silky sea. Some chiffon seaweeds, embroidered and ruched with metallic threads, have silk-bound wire roots anchoring into the sea. Frayed chiffon, stitched around fine wire, is twisted and caught in undulating patterns across the work's surface.

This work is then set against another 'sea of work', a sheer cloth against which bubbles of heat-distorted organza, silk seaweeds, semi-precious stones and seed pearls have been stitched, hence the sea deepens.

Towards the top of the piece the seaweeds become lighter and more translucent. A wire stitched through their centres enables me to undulate them as I stitch them into place, capturing space and suggesting depth.

Deep at the bottom of the sea the detail is denser, weighting the composition of the piece and the fabric itself. Bubbles of heat-distorted organza, seed pearls and chips of semi-precious stone are tangled with silk and crystal organza weeds.

Bubbled (heat-distorted) crystal organza and seaweeds cut from hand-painted silk deepen the sea through which the mermaid swims.

Autumn Reflection

It is late August when the alchemy begins. Golden tints appear in the hedgerows and trees. Crops ripen and shimmer in the sun. Summer yields gracefully to autumn.

Lustre-glossed berries hang sweet and heavy from bramble and bine. Drunken, brawling wasps spark like embers from russet, ripened, fermenting fruits, and drowsy bees nuzzle late summer blooms. Along the quiet lanes, butterflies dance between patches of honeyed light. It is the sunset of the year.

Tangled into the hedgerows and along the roadsides stand stems of parsleys, once misted with dainty white flowers, their now brittle, burnished umbels make hammocks for delicate spiders' webs and gather autumn mists which hang from them like jewels.

A single stem of cow parsley stands in relief in the foreground of the piece. Beyond this central stem lie two further sheer silk organza panels, one glimpsed through the next. The lacy gold cloth surrounding the piece is worked by machine stitching gold threads over cold-water soluble material which is ultimately dissolved away from the stitches. Further delicate leaves and tiny black satin seeds are caught into the tangle of stitches. My imagination translates the gold, bronze and jade green of turning leaves, the ruby and jet of ripening berries and the amber of ripened hazel and chestnuts into treasure. But, moreover, the real treasure of the season lies in tiny seeds such as these which nature carefully buries to yield another spring. Finally, the signature of the piece – a butterfly – rests on its border.

Autumn Reflection
40 x 64cm (16 x 25in)
The golden light of autumn inspired this study of cow parsley, standing brittle and burnished by the sun against a tangled hedgerow background.

UMBELS & LEAVES

The three-dimensional cow parsley in the foreground of the piece is constructed from silk-bound wire graduated to taper into the finer stems of the umbels. The silk binding thread is teased out at the end of each of these umbrella-like spokes to emulate the plant's delicate flower stems. The stem is then brushed with bronze silk paint. Tiny silk satin seeds are attached to the finest tips of the umbels. Finely cut leaves of soft green and bronze silk are bound into the stem with the fine wire stitched through their mid-veins.

The moss green seeds or fruit of an umbellifera, beautifully cupped in magenta umbels.

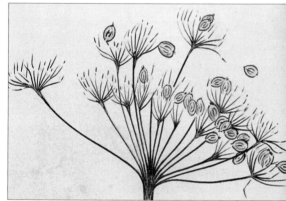

A working sketch of hogweed drawn on to calico using fabric pen and coloured with silk dye.

Cow parsley umbels, burnished bronze by a summer in the sun, tangle into the hedgerow.

86

BACKGROUND

Two silk organza panels illustrate the tangled hedgerow background of the study. The furthest panel is set back approximately 1cm (½in) and rests against a mirror. This construct creates the illusion of depth and encourages the eyes to rest, gaze and reflect within the piece. Both panels are dapple-dyed in autumnal shades, painted with stems of cow parsley and delicately embroidered with silk and gold threads.

The autumnal hedgerow background, scattered with silk satin cow parsley seeds and glinting with hand-embroidered gold threads.

BUTTERFLY

A butterfly with hand-painted silk and feather wings rests on a lacy cloth surrounding the piece. Its wings' intricate patterning is cut away using fine-pointed scissors to reveal a layer of feather beneath. This patterning is then traced around with gold thread, carefully couched into place with minute silk stitches.

The butterfly has a sleeky, frayed silk body, its antennae are feather fronds and its eyes jet black seeds. The lacy cloth upon which it rests is worked by machine stitching gold threads over cold-water soluble material which is ultimately dissolved away from the stitches. Delicate, silk cow parsley leaves and true-to-nature, heart-shaped seeds are scattered across the lacy cloth and stitched invisibly where they fall.

A butterfly, the signature of the piece, rests at its corner.

Through the seasons

Spring, summer, autumn and winter; the plants of the umbellifera family hold themselves up against the changing seasons like delicate umbrellas.

In springtime, Queen Anne's lace graces the lanes and verges of the countryside, its dainty white flowers seemingly hanging like a mist above the complex tangle of fern-like leaves and delicate stems upon which they are borne. Sweet cicely flowers in unison, once prized for its sweet aroma and flavour of aniseed. Then follow hedge parsley, saxifrage, angelica, hemlock and hogweed and many, many more, each with characteristic umbels or 'umbrellas' of flowers. They hold their floral canopies on graceful stems with a certain poise, a sense of occasion – their season, only to be collapsed or unfurled by the season itself.

Their dainty flowers fall; fruits, then seeds, follow. As the year progresses only the brittle, burnished stems of the later-flowering species remain. Throughout the autumn, their umbrella-like ribs cradle spiders' webs, gathering the season's soft mists which hang there like fairylights sparkling in the sun. In winter, the few remaining stems sparkle with frost like the giant wands of wizards.

I worked these three studies reflecting on the habit of the beautiful umbelliferae throughout the seasons. I used the device of a window against which I could, season by season, project respectively the flower, burnished umbels and frosted stems, and a border against which I could set details.

Through the Seasons
Spring/Summer
30 x 40cm (12 x 16in)
The dainty white flowers of
Queen Anne's lace lie like mist
in countryside verges.

SPRING/SUMMER

I began my series of umbelliferae studies with Queen Anne's lace – one of the earliest of the cow parsley family to grace countryside verges.

Impressionistically I painted its dainty white flowers, delicate stems and fern-like leaves on to silk organza. Stretching the silk painting taut behind the window framing the study, I carefully detailed the stems in silk stem stitch. I applied delicate leaves cut from hand-painted silk and wired through their mid-veins, lifting them away from the work's surface to create dimension. I then embellished the flower heads with fragments of silk satin, catching them down with bullion knots and seed stitches. I caught further silk fragments on to stiffened silk flower stems and stitched them in to fall away from the work's surface, securing them only at their base, thus giving each miniature umbel more form. I surrounded the study with a lacy cloth of silk threads worked on to soluble fabric. Wiring its edges with silk-bound wire I then manipulated it to gently undulate away from the work's surface, capturing space, or the illusion thereof.

The window frame is a collage of silk threads, fabric wisps and pressed cow parsley leaves burnished with gold and bronze metallic powders. Against it are set lacewings with embroidered silk wings, a butterfly and a scattering of cow parsley leaves.

Swatch exploring the materials used for Spring/Summer.

The butterfly's wings, spanning 4.5cm (1¾in), are of hand-painted silk and feather, the silk being cut away to reveal the feather beneath. This patterning is then traced around with a fine gold thread held into place with silk stitches.

90

A close-up of the fern-like leaves of the cow parsley.

A magnified detail of the soft white flower heads of the cow parsley.

AUTUMN

The autumn study has a window obscured by a lacy cloth of metallic stitches worked over soluble fabric, set against silk chiffon. Beyond this, at a distance of approximately 5cm (2in), a mirror catches its reflection together with that of a stem of cow parsley. Against the mount rest a turquoise moth, a beetle and a lacewing.

Photographs of umbelliferae in the autumn.

Through the Seasons
Autumn
25.5 x 31.5cm (10 x 12in)
Once verdant green stems now stand brittle and bronzed by a summer's sun.

93

UMBELS & LEAVES

The plant's stem is constructed from silk-bound wire graduated in thickness and divided into branches. The wrapping thread is gently teased out at the end of each of these branches to emulate the plant's delicate flower stems or umbels. The stems are then dry brushed with bronze silk paint and scattered with tiny, heart-shaped seeds cut from black silk satin. The finely divided, toothed leaves are cut from silk habotai, softly shaded with bronze and green. Wires are minutely stitched through their mid-veins before they are drawn together and bound into the main stem.

The mount surrounding the window against which the stem of cow parsley stands is a collage of fabric, thread and silk fibres burnished with bronze and copper metallic powders.

Cow parsley umbels, bare of their dainty white flowers and verdant green leaves, are represented here as they stand in nature – like the spokes of miniature umbrellas, bereft of their silk!

BEETLE

The beetle has a body covered in fragments of silk minutely stitched into place and detailed with couched gold thread. Its legs are bound wire, its eyes are seeds and antennae feather fronds.

A tiny turquoise beetle, no bigger than the tip of my little finger.

94

MOTH

The moth has hand-painted, layered silk wings, the top layer being cut away to reveal its vibrant turquoise eyes, or patterning, which is then traced around with a fine gold thread carefully couched into place with minute stitches.

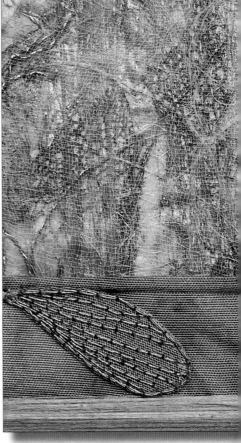

The moth's turquoise wings are in perfect contrast to the copper- and bronze-coloured border upon which it rests. Unlike its counterpart in nature, it chooses not to be camouflaged … no fear of predators in a work of art!

LACEWING

The lacewing has dappled bronze organza wings veined with copper thread, couched into place with silk stitches. Its body and diminutive legs are bound wire, its eyes are seeds and its antennae are feather fronds. Burnished silk leaves tumble across the mount, carefully secured where they naturally fall with single knotted stitches.

The lacewing merges naturalistically into the border upon which it rests. In my observation, lacewings fade naturally from vibrant green to more coppery tones as the year progresses.

WINTER

I reflect upon the qualities of winter in the third and final study. A solitary stem – or miniature wizard's wand – stands against an isolated window, frosted silver. The piece measures just 23cm (9in) high … the scale of the giant hogweed that inspired it, being 3.5m (12ft) high, I sensibly considered to be a little ambitious to emulate!

The stem of hogweed in this piece was constructed very similarly to the stem of cow parsley in the autumn study. The window against which it stands holds a very sheer piece of chiffon on to which I have caught fragments of fine, metal-weave fabric, sheer, silvery chiffon and shimmery, lightweight organza. I took long, unbroken stitches in silver thread to impart a jagged feel. I also stitched some chips of semi-precious stone across the chiffon to twinkle, frosty bright. A delicate spider's web is caught in the corner of the window frame. The border surrounding the mirror is a collage of silk fibres and threads burnished with metallic silver powder. Against it rests a member of the silk cranefly species. It has a silk-bound body and legs, and jet black seeds for eyes. Its wings are delicately embroidered with silver and silk thread.

Finally, the window is set against a mirror, reflecting details of the work within the piece and any light falling on it.

**Through the Seasons
Winter**

Shown actual size.
The smallest of the
three studies. This
winter reflection bears
a miniature stem
of hogweed, barely
25.5cm (10in) high, its
counterpart in nature
growing to in excess of
3.5m (12ft)!

97

CRANEFLY & COBWEB

Against the border surrounding the window rests a member of the silk cranefly species (far from botanically correct in any detail!). It has a silk-bound body and legs, and jet black seeds for eyes. Its wings are delicately embroidered with silver and silk thread.

A delicate spider's web is woven across the corner of the window frame. Using very fine silk thread, I drew stitches across the corner of the frame. Taking my needle to the centre of this criss-cross web, I wove in and out of the threads, knotting as I worked … very carefully and quietly … quite in awe of the spider whose web I aspired to suggest with human hands and silk thread!

Dew caught on a spider's web sparkles like fairylights in the early morning sun.

The spindly, silk-bound legs of the cranefly stretch out across the frosty silver frame against which it rests, as if barely holding him from slipping.

98

UMBEL

The stem of hogweed in this piece was constructed very similarly to the stem of cow parsley in the autumn study: using silk-bound wire, graduated in thickness and divided into branches, or umbels, the binding thread being teased out at the ends of the branching wires to emulate the delicate flower stems of the plant. I painted the resolved stem with blond and silver fabric paint, adding touches of metallic silver powder.

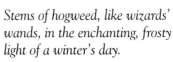

A miniature stem of hogweed, created from silk and wire.

Stems of hogweed, like wizards' wands, in the enchanting, frosty light of a winter's day.

Daisies

A window surrounded by a deep border holds a picture of daisies painted on to sheer silk organza and embroidered with both flat and plied silk threads. The silk organza on to which the daisies are painted allows a mirror fixed behind it to reflect through, giving extra depth to the piece.

French knots lie at the centre of each flower surrounded by rays of tiny satin petals cut with fine scissors and secured with invisible stitches. The soft grass amidst which the daisies are set is painted on to the backcloth before being detailed with stem stitch in plied silk floss. The spoon-shaped leaves are likewise painted on to the backcloth but left unembroidered so as not to dominate the picture. The picture is then diffused with an overlay of sheer chiffon sponged with pearlescent dyes.

The grass green border echoes the design of ancient illuminated manuscripts. It is cut from mount board before being covered with silk fibres and painted with silk dyes and iridescent pigments. Silk satin petals are scattered across it and three dainty, three-dimensional daisies and a butterfly rest on its surface. The daisies have silk petals gathered around frayed silk centres and bound on to silk-covered wire stems. Each daisy petal is touched faintly pink at its edges with a dry brush barely dipped in dye. The butterfly has silk wings, hand-painted and patterned with pure gold and silk embroidery. Its body is frayed silk, its antennae are feather fronds and its eyes are tiny seeds.

Daisies
22 x 30cm (8 x 12in)
A daisy miniature,
reflecting on the dainty
nature of the flower.

Mayweed bordering Home Field, Chettle, Dorset.

DAISIES

Magnified here, the miniature French knots at the centre of each flower can be seen clearly. Likewise, the applied silk satin petals and stem stitch detailing the grasses. The pearlescent colour floating across the daisy painting, carried on a piece of very sheer chiffon, mists and softens the whole composition.

Daisies, pictured in the window of the study.

BUTTERFLY

A dainty, soft, green butterfly rests at the corner of this daisy study. Its wings are cut from a papery cloth of silk fibres and painted with silk dyes. Their patterning is traced with gold thread, couched with tiny silk stitches. Its body is frayed silk, its eyes are tiny seeds and its antennae feather fronds.

A butterfly with delicate silk wings embroidered with fine silk and pure gold thread rests at the corner of the window frame.

Daisy Chain

Daisy chains, if not the memory or pleasure of making them, fade; hence the inspiration to make one which will not.

Particularly on mowing days, before the petrol was poured into the lawn mower's tank and the 'fierce monster' roared into life, I would 'save' as many daisies as possible; fill egg cups and dollies' tea cups with water and rest them there. Some would become daisy chains. I would pinch their fleshy stems and thread them together to make necklaces, crowns, garlands and ribbons. I can remember how testing it could be with tiny short fingernails to pinch a fine-enough hole for threading. Many stems became shorter and shorter as I bruised my way up towards the flower head to start again! It is a joy to have long, 'grown-up' fingernails now, without the grown-up attitude which might prevent me from playing. A child then, a child now!

The daisies in this chain have cut silk petals painted with pearlised dye. Many are tinted pink at their edges, as in nature. They are attached around stamens of frayed silk and wrapped with a calyx of fine bonded cloth, stretched to fit snugly. Their stems are silk-bound wire; two wires are bound together, then parted, bound separately and rejoined to create the tiny pinched hole through which the chain is threaded.

Winter Reflection

Winter is like a secret, whispered into the wind, silently held. Nature itself keeps it, in the eerie silence of the bare beech woods and the blue shadows cast by the winter sun.

It is a secret that stills the earth, freezes the air, brings snow and ice, yet it is not of great portent, it has the spirit of an inaudible prayer. Share the secret, imbibe the mystery and celebrate the winter. Catch a feather on the wind. Catch the wintry sunlight on your face. Reflect; this is the very beginning not the end. This is a new year dawning. Sense the frozen earth yielding then watch the first flowers opening. The secret, the mystery, the miracle, is new life.

Winter sunlight sparkled against the window of our village church. I gazed into it until it began to dance behind my eyes, to lighten my mood. It gathered into the shape of an angel in my imagination and became my meditation.

As the light slowly faded my meditation was broken, but there remained a feather, caught in some wire mesh drawn protectively across the surface of the glass. It seemed to me that it had been blown there on the breath of God; an angel's feather. Pulling it free I brushed it across my face and felt blessed.

As I stepped back from the window I noticed a delicate snowdrop flowering in a sheltered corner against the church wall; earlier than I had ever known them flower before.

This quiet, reflective time became the inspiration behind this piece.

St Marys Church, Chettle, Dorset.

104

Swatch exploring the materials
used in Winter Reflection.

Winter Reflection
28 x 94cm (11 x 37in)
A white feather is caught into the stitched
mesh at the base of the window along with
a delicate silk feather. At the opposite corner
two three-dimensional snowdrops with hand-
painted silk petals and leaves and silk-bound
stems gracefully nod their heads.

BACKGROUND & FRAME

The arched window frame is cut from heavy linen canvas, painted silver and covered with fragments of metallic fabric and blue, grey and green silk. They are held in place with wavy lines of surface stitches in sheeny dark blue and metallic threads. This surface is then covered with a lacy cloth of silver threads worked over cold-water soluble fabric. The arch and the outside edges of the piece are defined with heavy silver thread couched down with fine silver thread. The 'glass' is fine silk organza sponge-dyed with iridescent silver fabric paint. It is scored with a blade and layered with silk tulle and further fragments of organza and stitched with fine metallic and silk threads.

A stitched pattern of abstracted diamonds echoes the pattern of the church glass. This diamond pattern is further identified with the surface application of organza and metal-weave fabric diamonds. The scoring and broken stitching suggest the fragility of the ancient glass in the delicate, frosty light of winter; a quality further enhanced by the positioning of a mirror at the back of the box frame upon which the whole piece is mounted. The delicate reflection of the stitching is glimpsed through the sheer organza, the silvery quality of the mirror illuminating the whole piece.

The fragmented wire mesh covering the window is represented with a mesh of stitches worked over cold-water soluble fabric then delicately and loosely stitched into place. The mesh is also patterned directly on to the organza in fragmented sections, hand stitched in steel blue silk thread.

The window pane and the border surrounding it are intricately layered and stitched. Sheer and metallic fabrics are used to describe the glass; heavier-weave fabrics overlaid with more delicate fabrics describe the surround. Many stitches are worked directly into the fabric of the window and surround. Others, such as the lacy stitches covering the surround and those describing the wire mesh, are worked over cold-water soluble fabric before being overlaid on to the piece and stitched into place.

ANGEL

An angel rests at the top of the window. She has open wings, a wispy body, delicate silk hair and softly defined features. Her feathers are cut from frayed silk ribbons, each feather being cut individually and carefully stitched into place against her blue silk organza silhouette. Wisps of real feather down are layered in with the silk feathers. Her body is covered with soft feather fronds and detailed with gold feather stitch. Her torso, face and hair are detailed with hand stitching in gold and silk. She has a soft gold halo of metal-weave fabric.

The angel's feathers are cut from hand-painted, frayed silk ribbons and individually stitched on to a silk organza silhouette of her wings. Wisps of feather down are caught amongst them, again secured with minute stitches.

A softly defined angel with silk feathered wings takes flight in my imagination. A likeness is caught in the silvery reflection of a window pane, her outstretched wings, a subtle form, echo the cool blue light of a winter's day.

Wisps of silk and feather down surround the angel's face. Golden hair falls from her crown, delicately and invisibly caught into place with fine silk stitches. Her expression is detailed in fine gold thread couched down with silk stitches. A halo of metal-weave fabric surrounds her, stitched almost invisibly with a thread drawn from the metal-weave fabric itself.

107

Dragonfly Dance

Enchanted at the water's edge, my spirit dances with the flight of the dragonfly. Every ripple of this gentle stream reflects its light. Its darting body, an emerald wand, has cast a certain spell on me. A spell which grants me eyes to see pure gold amongst the reeds, forget-me-nots as sapphires at my feet, to feel the sun as a tender kiss and hear peace whispered in the breeze.

I began this piece reflecting on the colour and light of an enchantingly beautiful dragonfly that I had spent a spell of time watching one July afternoon. Its wings, sheer gossamer, shining full of light, its body emerald green and sapphire blue, dazzlingly bright.

I looked out my gossamer silk tops and iridescent dyes and began making a papery dragonfly cloth. Teasing out the silk fibres and laying them down in a large sheet, I dappled them with colour and held them together with dilute glue.

Having achieved my dragonfly cloth, I bordered it with an emerald green frame, itself bound in silk fibres, and worked with iridescent dyes and metallic powders.

I stitched reeds in sheeny silk threads dividing the stream in the foreground from the sky above, then I began depicting the dragonfly. Tracing the shape of its darting body in pure gold thread, I couched it down with tiny silk stitches, leaving the thread trailing as if dancing away from its tail to suggest movement. Its eyes are chips of emerald caught within the couched gold thread. Its legs are miniature lengths of wire bound with gold thread and bent into shape. Its wings are cut from very fine silk paper, worked in a similar way to the dragonfly cloth, their veining patterned with pure gold thread couched into place with tiny silk stitches. I echoed the shape of the wings against the sky with pale gold silk stitches to emphasise movement.

The reeds in the foreground were both painted directly on to the dragonfly cloth and applied three-dimensionally. Those painted into place were then detailed with silk stitches. The three-dimensional reeds were cut from silk chiffon and shimmering organza before being wired through their mid-veins to give them form and strength. They were then stitched securely into place within and against the emerald green frame.

Three dainty moths climb the reeds. They have hand-painted, layered silk wings, cut away to reveal vibrant turquoise eyes or patterning, which is traced around with a fine gold thread carefully couched into place with minute silk stitches.

Water forget-me-nots, standing by the stream-washed shore, seem to reflect the clear, unbroken skies of July. A vibrant yellow eye at the centre of each open flower seems to intensify their sky blue, as does the pinched pink of the unopened buds, clustered towards the tip of each gracefully arched stem.

Dragonfly Dance
86 x 134cm (34 x 53in)
A dragonfly dances into the shimmering light of a summer's day. Beside the stream, water forget-me-nots flourish amidst glossy water reeds. Moths, sleepy by day, rest their wings in the dappled shade.

Delicate dragonfly wings cut from papery silk cloth and embroidered with gold thread.

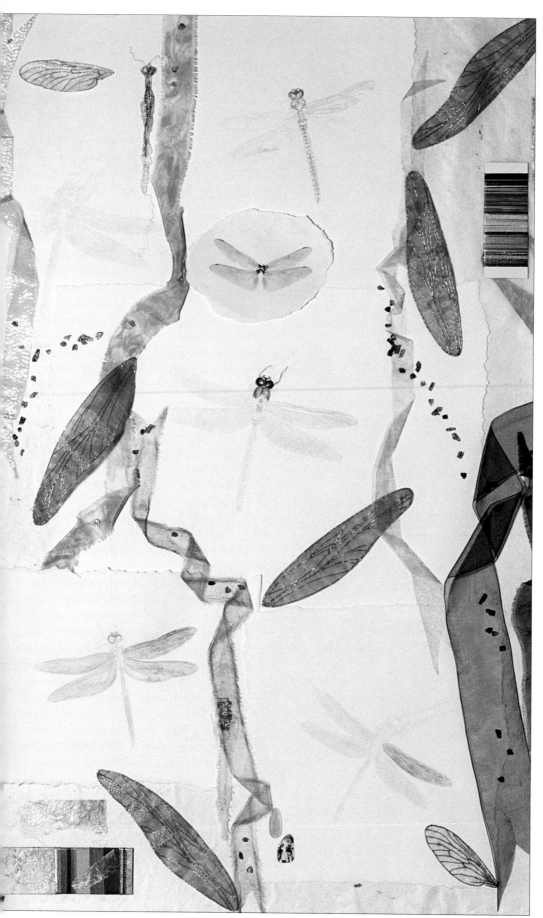

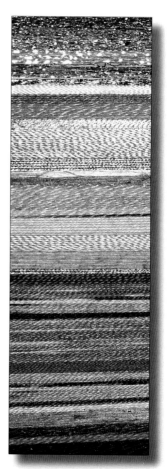

Thread swatch for Dragonfly Dance.

Storyboard, exploring the inspiration and the materials used for Dragonfly Dance.

STREAM

I worked the reeds in the mid-distance with plied and unplied silk floss in a spectrum of greens, deepest bottle glass to lightest gold, taking long stitches, sheeny in their unbroken length. I caught the light on the water with horizontal runs of stitches in metallic blue and silk threads.

One July afternoon at the water's edge, Wardour Lake, Dorset.

Reeds stitched in sheeny floss silk divide the stream in the foreground from the sky above.

DRAGONFLY

Quiet, but for the applause
of the dragonfly's wings.
Still, but for his dance.
Gazing, yet focused,
entranced by his emerald
shimmer.
Awake, yet sleeping.
Musing and drifting,
dragonfly dreaming.

The dragonfly, with its embroidered, papery silk wings and darting body of pure gold and silk thread.

111

FORGET-ME-NOTS

My forget-me-nots, in the very foreground of the piece, have silk-bound stems, flowering with sky blue silk flowers. Hand-painted and individually cut, they have bright yellow silk bullion knots at their centres by which they are attached to the stem of the plant. Tiny, pinched, pink silk buds are bound on to each arching stem with green silk floss. The cut silk leaves are wired through their mid-veins before being carefully bound on to the stem with silk floss.

The water forget-me-nots, described in silk.

MOTHS

Three dainty moths climb the reeds in the foreground of the piece. They have hand-painted, layered silk wings, their patterning being cut away from the surface layer to reveal their vibrant turquoise blue underwings. This patterning is then traced around with a very fine gold thread couched down with tiny silk stitches. Their bodies, which are of frayed silk, are the same vibrant blue of their underwings. They have miniature golden eyes and delicate feather antennae. They each have six tiny, silk-bound wire legs with which they climb the silk organza reeds.

One of the moths rests above my signature, stitched in gold thread.

Resting on the reeds, sleepy by day (I quote from my imagination). This silken-winged moth is gripped securely by its tiny silk- and gold-bound legs.

A chalk hill blue butterfly.

Sunlight

One dreary February day, I coaxed myself out of a grey mindset and into my walking boots. Making my way into a deep thicket, through shiny green ivy and ground elder, my spirits began to lift. My steps drew a cool, earthy, green scent into the air. My eyes relaxed their focus and gazed, allowing my mind to drift. With each step I moved further away from anxiety, deeper into a new reality. The day's light began to lift, casting faint shadows through the bony winter branches of oak and hazel. Then, in a gentle hollow, I saw a pool of sunshine, not cast from the still, soft grey sky, but flowering from the earth: aconites.

A passage from my diary quotes the inspiration for this piece, worked in honour of the winter-flowering aconite. Intricately hand-stitched it is worked in a variety of hand-painted silks, pure gold and floss threads.

The cloth supporting the three-dimensional detail of the piece is extremely sheer chiffon, achieved by removing many of the cloth's original warp and weft threads, creating the illusion of 'nothing', of space, whilst providing an anchor for the work.

The aconites have strong stems of silk-bound wire, bearing heads of silk dupion petals, with knotted and frayed silk stamens. A ruffle of silk leaves, wired for support, surround each flower head. Each flower is carefully and securely stitched against the sheer backcloth and manipulated to imitate life. Beneath the aconites lie fallen leaves cut from hand-painted silk and embroidered with gold and silk thread. Fine, bound wire and gold thread represent the imagined roots of the aconites tumbling through the undergrowth. Frayed silk snippets, invisibly caught on to the backcloth with tiny stitches, suggest moss.

The butterflies within the piece have wings patterned with pure gold thread, couched into place with tiny silk stitches. Their bodies are of frayed silk; their eyes are tiny seeds and their antennae feather fronds. One pauses for nectar amidst the flowers; two fly against the misty chiffon sky.

There is a second panel of painted organza, behind the sheer chiffon, on to which I have stitched the radiating patterns of the aconite leaves, suggestive of rays of sunlight. Behind this there is a mirror reflecting light within the piece.

The winter-flowering aconite, Eranthis hyemalis.

Sunlight
28 x 46cm (11 x 18in)
The winter-flowering aconite, with its sunshine-
yellow flowers and leafy green bracts, in pattern
like miniature sunburst, brings the joy of a warm,
sunny day to my heart when I discover it flowering
in the still, wintry woodlands surrounding my
home in Dorset.

ACONITES

Oak leaves cut from various weights of hand-painted silk detailed with gold and silk thread lie beneath the aconite. Carefully under-wired and manipulated to tumble against each other, they emulate the woodland floor. Wispy, green silk is caught amongst them to suggest moss. The imagined golden roots of the aconites, made from wire bound with gold thread, twine into their silken woodland world.

The imagined golden roots of the aconites twine amongst the fallen leaves of the undergrowth.

Returning from a walk, I used my walking boot to rest the dainty bunch of aconites, snowdrops and catkins I had gathered to study.

BUTTERFLIES

Two butterflies with hand-embroidered wings and shimmery silk bodies are caught against the all-but-invisible chiffon supporting the piece. Beyond this chiffon sky, at a distance of approximately 4cm (1½in), lies another panel of silk organza embroidered with the radiating sunburst pattern of the aconite bracts. Beyond this a mirror imparts its reflective quality to the piece.

A butterfly takes to the chiffon sky.

Another butterfly rests amidst the aconites, sunning its embroidered silk wings. The process of securing the delicate details of my work in place calls for an equally delicate hand. Many times I quite literally take a deep breath, holding it as I draw the needle through the details that I am stitching, subconsciously believing that this internal poise reaches beyond me to become instilled into the finished work. It is curious to reflect that I often find myself quite breathless whilst pursuing an essentially sedentary goal.

Day Spring

A warm May breeze, as gentle as a sigh, moves through grassy verges and steep banks profuse with flowers; stitchwort and campion, herb Robert, wood anemones and speedwell curtsy and sway, and I am moved to sit amongst them and dream, my sigh contentment.

To pause amongst the flowers of May is to me, as it is to butterflies newly emerged from their hibernation, 'nectar'. To see, to truly see, not just in passing by but in pausing, the beauty that surrounds us is to glimpse Eden. So many species flowering together in the halo light of a new year, their colours dancing, their scent imperceptibly beckoning, is the very definition of joy.

I worked this piece over the course of five months; delighting in each flower, carefully studying their every detail, beginning with the wood anemone, or 'wind flower'.

Germander speedwell,
Veronica chamaedrys,
growing amongst vetch.

Greater stitchwort, Stellaria holostea.

Day Spring
38 x 68cm (15 x 27in)
'In winter the earth draws in
her breath, in spring lets out
a gentle sigh'.
Delighting in the flowers of
spring, I began this study
with the first to flower;
wood anemones. Spring
had yielded to summer long
before I had taken the final
stitches at the centre of the
campion flowers.

ANEMONES (WIND FLOWERS)

The name 'wind flower' is derived from the ancient Greek understanding that the petals only open when the wind blows. A plant, then, that surely waits for the 'gentle sigh of spring'. The flowers only open wide on sunny days, closing and nodding gracefully near evening; shy of cloudy days, their pink- or lilac-blushed petals remain closed. Seemingly fragile, they are in fact able to withstand the most blustery of spring days.

I individually cut and painted the silk petals of the anemones in this piece, controlling very carefully the 'blush' to each, and wired them to impart their natural strength, sewing very fine wire into place through their centres with even finer thread. In this study, the sun is shining and all the anemones' faces are upturned. Clustered at their centres are frayed silk and knotted silk stamens. The petals and stamens are bound to wire stems. About a third of the way down each slender stem is a ring of three leaves, each divided into three toothed segments. These leaves are cut from hand-painted silk and wired through their centres on to the central stem. They stand their silk-covered ground in anticipation of the flowers to follow.

The wood anemone, or wind flower,
Anemone nemorosa.

The anemones are open wide, as if on a sunny day.

The anemone petals, faintly blushed with pink
silk paint, each have a fine wire delicately
stitched through their centres.

120

STITCHWORT

Next to flourish creatively was stitchwort with its long, fragile stems and deeply divided, dainty, white petals. At the centre of each flower is a silk-covered bead interpreting what in nature develops into the seed-bearing fruit of the plant.

In preparing to work my stems of stitchwort, I picked several, sketching them initially, then having them by me as I made my three-dimensional interpretation, in the course of which several of these fruits matured into perfect miniature green globes. As the seeds ripened within and the globes became dry and papery they rattled, which delighted me! I eventually returned the stems to nature just outside my studio door where I hope they will grow and delight in perpetuity.

Around each silk-covered bead I caught knotted and frayed silk stamens; into their centres I stitched white silk 'styles'. Five silk satin petals are attached to each. They are bound on to silk-covered wire stems with green calyxes cut from fine bonded cloth. The flower stems, some of which carry tiny, pinched silk buds, have tiny, green, silk leaves bound in along their length. They are drawn together on to a heavier silk-bound wire in groups of three. At this point, narrow leaves cut from fine painted silk and wired through their centres with a very fine wire are attached. This point is very fragile in nature, easily snapping.

Emulating it presented quite a challenge to me. Determined to honour its natural delicacy, it was indeed a delicate process. These stems are gathered again into groups of three and brought together at another delicate junction with a slightly heavier silk-covered wire stem.

Further narrow, pointed leaves are attached here and further down the stem towards the silk-covered ground.

A pencil and watercolour sketch.

Greater stitchwort,
Stellaria holostea.

The dainty flowers of the greater stitchwort, portrayed in silk.

The stitchwort stems are very delicate, needing the support of other hedgerow flowers. Red campion provides such support within this composition.

RED CAMPION

In nature, the delicate stitchwort needs the support of other flowers and grasses to thrive. In my study this support is found in stems of campion, a much stronger plant, which thrives in verges and hedgerows and has even been known to climb mountains and establish itself in crevices and on cliff edges.

Flower heads with wired silk petals and knotted silk stamens are attached to strong, silk-covered wire stems, with snug, green, silk calyxes. Pinched silk buds, wizened flowers and finely wired leaflets are bound into place appropriately. Each flower stem has several junctions where the weight of the wire is altered to emulate nature; each junction bears further leaves graduating in size.

Red campion, Silene dioica.

In this magnified photograph you can see the minute stitches along the length of each petal and the individually knotted silk stamens at the centre of each flower.

A plant study, carefully considering petal length, the number of leaves, leaflets, petals, stamens, buds and seed heads of a stem of red campion.

A silk painting of red campion.

A watercolour and pencil sketch of red campion.

HERB ROBERT

Herb Robert echoes the pink of the campion with its rounded pink petals and pink-tinged, serrated leaves which, as the plant fades towards autumn, turn fiery red. Its petals are cut from pink silk wired through their centres and attached to silk-bound wire stems. Frayed silk stamens are clustered at the centre of each. Their cut silk leaves tinged pinky bronze are attached to long, silk-bound wire stems and joined to the flowering stem in the habit of the plant. The seed heads are worked from silk-bound beads and feather quill.

The dainty flower of herb Robert, Geranium robertianum. *Each tiny silk petal is carefully hand-painted.*

SPEEDWELL

Finally, bright, blue-eyed speedwell peer out of the foliage at the base of the piece. Its growing season is slightly longer than that of its companions in this piece, therefore I worked it last; planting it into the green silk base I wove it through their stems, resting it in the undergrowth. Its flowers have four attached petals which I painted individually with a fine brush to achieve their subtle, sky blue/cloud white variation. The lower of the four petals is narrower than the others, which I was careful to quote. Each flower has only two stamens; I used knotted silk, stitching it through each flower centre before binding them to wire stems with silk calyxes and silk floss. The leaves are cut from silk, wired through their mid-veins and attached to the stems in the habit of the plant.

Germander speedwell, Veronica chamaedrys.

Blue-eyed speedwell, with hand-painted silk petals, climbs through the stems of the anemones, stitchwort, campion and herb Robert.

BUTTERFLIES

Three butterflies pause amongst the flowers, just as I did. Their wings are cut from the same painted silk as the campion petals. Their delicate veining is traced in pure gold and silk thread couched into place with tiny stitches. They are invisibly wired, enabling me to lift them to rest naturalistically as if pausing from flight. Their bodies are frayed silk, the deep maroon of the herb Robert stems. Their eyes are tiny seeds, their antennae feather fronds.

A butterfly, with painted silk wings embroidered with silk and gold thread, pauses amongst the spring flowers.

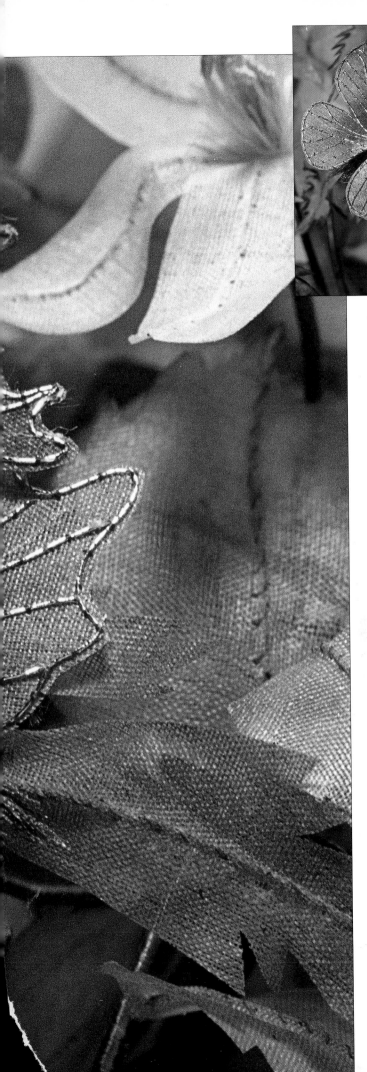

A butterfly rests on the pink-tinged leaves of the herb Robert, its wings in colour harmony.

Orange tip butterfly on red campion.

A butterfly pauses in the midst of wind flowers and speedwell.

127

INDEX